C000180773

RECOVERY VEHICLES

First published in1998 by
Roundoak Publishing
The Old Dairy,
East Nynehead,
Wellington,
Somerset, England
TA21 ODA

Tel. 01823 461997
Fax 01823 461998

All rights reserved.
No part of this publication may be produced, stored in a retrieval system or transmitted in any form by any means electronic, mechanical, optical, photocopying, recording or otherwise without the prior written agreement of the publisher.

© Copyright 1998
Mick Waite &
Roundoak Publishing
ISBN 1-871565-30-8

Design by
Roundoak Associates

Printed in Great Britain by
**The Amadeus Press,
Huddersfield, West Yorkshire**

Front cover and left: Egerton's S41 steel sleeper cabbed vehicle was for many years based on the North bound service area at Sandbach on the M6 where this photograph was taken. The body stylist has taken great care to blend the front panel of the body with the sloping rear panel of the cab to create a pleasing appearance. The truck was sold on in the early Nineties.

Rear cover: JDS's Renault has been fitted with the latest type one-piece front grille and a modified front bumper to give it a more up to date appearance. Now only used to complement the workshop services provided by the Blackburn depot, it still remains a vital part of the company's commitment to customer service and repair.

RECOVERY VEHICLES

Mick Waite

Roundoak Publishing

ACKNOWLEDGEMENTS

This book is not meant to be a definitive history of the recovery vehicle but merely a chance to share part of a photograph collection amassed over a period of twenty years.

I make no apologies for including several vehicles from the same fleet as the individuality of the recovery vehicle means that operators are inclined to own trucks built for a specific task, utilising whatever equipment and chassis are available at the time.

I would like to pass on my sincere thanks to the many owners and operators who have found time to provide me with the information included in the captions, all of which was provided in good faith.

I would also like to thank the following people :-

My wife Debbie and children, Samantha and Daniel.

Kevin Cobb, Peter Davies, Les Freathy, David Lee, Marcus Lester, David Stretton, Richard Tew, John Wynn and especially David Weston for supplying some of the photographs.

Alan at Newtyle Commercials.

Wards of Burnley.

JDS Trucks.

Mick Waite

Brierfield, Nelson,
Lancs.
February 1998

GLOSSARY OF TERMS

FLYER
A raised pedestal upon which the work lamps and flashing amber lights are mounted.

SNATCH BLOCK
A pulley block around which the winch rope is fed in order to change the direction of pull, or to increase the mechanical advantage of the winch.

STROP
A wide nylon based strap that is passed around a casualty to allow it to be lifted, pulled or rolled without causing further damage.

LIGHT BAR
A housing that contains more than one flashing light and is available in various widths with numerous combinations of lights.

CASUALTY
A broken down or accident damaged vehicle.

JIB OR BOOM
The main lifting structure of a crane.

SPADES
Hydraulic blades that dig into the ground to prevent a recovery vehicle being pulled backwards when winching.

STIFF LEGS
Supports that are lowered to the ground to stabilise a vehicle during lifting operations.

GROSS TRAIN WEIGHT (G.T.W.)
The maximum combined weight of a motor vehicle and any trailer towed by it, i.e. a recovery vehicle plus casualty.

GROSS VEHICLE WEIGHT (G.V.W.)
The maximum weight of a laden motor vehicle.

R.R.R.A.
The Road Rescue & Recovery Association.

A.V.R.O.
Association of Vehicle Recovery Operators.

INTRODUCTION

When motoring was in its infancy, the lack of knowledge and skill that was prevalent in the new motoring gentry ensured that breakdowns and accidents were plentiful. Many village blacksmiths realised this and turned their attentions away from the traditional crafts and became the saviours of the horseless carriage.

As many small workshops sprang up around the country, their proprietors sought ways of increasing and expanding their businesses. One option was to provide a breakdown and recovery service.

Many early towing vehicles were nothing more than a private car equipped with only a length of rope or chain. This is fine as long as the casualty is not damaged, and the driver being towed knows about stopping before he runs into the back of the towing vehicle. If the casualty was damaged, it may require lifting, so a light pick-up truck would be used. This would be fitted with a fabricated jib, on the end of which would be some form of hoist, usually a block and tackle, with which any lifting could be done.

The advent of the First World War saw the motor vehicle enter a new chapter in its development. The extensive use of motor transport saw many light trucks converted into crude recovery vehicles which were nothing more than local adaptations of civilian equipment because there was as yet no standardised military pattern recovery vehicle, or trained personnel.

At war's end many of these trucks found their way into civilian service with local garages and transport contractors who were eager to operate a breakdown and recovery service for their customers. However, the specialised equipment market was virtually non existent, most of what there was being home made by individual operators. In fact this is a trend that has lasted to this day albeit to a lesser extent.

A company called Harvey Frost started importing garage equipment from the U.S.A. and included in this range was a light vehicle salvage crane manufactured by the Weaver Corporation. So successful was this product that companies like Harvey Frost and Mann Egerton, who had seen the potential of these cranes, decided to manufacture their own variations. Mann Egerton even took the bold step of designing and building a tilting trailer, onto which a casualty could be winched and then transported away.

Right: An immaculate Wreckmaster equipped Ford Transcontinental from Welbourns Recovery of Wisbech. To complement the versatile twin boom, P & D Cosby of Kirton Holme, near Boston have fitted a Zacklift Z20 underlift unit which is specially designed to be fitted to existing recovery vehicles.

By the end of the 1930's the world was once again plunged into global conflict and again motor transport was at the forefront of military logistics. It was these times of conflict that gave the industry one of the best pieces of recovery hardware, the twin boom crane.

The Holmes twin boom was designed by Ernest Holmes around 1920 for use in his auto repair company. It consisted of two winch equipped booms that could be used independently, together, or swung out over the side to provide winch and lift facilities in a number of combinations. Such was the success of the design, that it was developed to cater for commercials as well as light cars and vans. The most famous of the early models was the W45. This was the model fitted to the Diamond T chassis and supplied to the Allied forces in great numbers during the conflict. These workhorses were to capture the hearts of recovery men the world over with their versatility and appetite for hard work. Many can still be found hard at work today. Over the years, the design and quality has been improved greatly, but the basic concept remains the same.

The years following the war were fruitful ones, but, with many demobbed military recovery vehicles available to civilian operators development of new equipment was very slow.

It was at this time that a Swedish engineer was developing a revolutionary new hydraulic recovery system that was about to take the world by storm, it was what we now know as the underlift. Brilliant in its design, it consists of a main boom or jib on the end of which is a drop arm. At the bottom of this drop arm is a hinged arm or foot which is extendable. Fitted to the end of this foot is a cross head onto which various attachments are placed. These are positioned under the casualty and provide lift from underneath, hence the name 'Underlift'.

The concept was established in the Scandinavian countries for many years before it became popular in the U.K., and likewise before it became popular in the U.S.A. Nowadays the underlift damage free system reigns supreme in the recovery industry.

Over the past few years, the recovery industry has gone through an immense change. Great efforts have been made to make the industry more professional in its attitude and application. Trade organisations such as the Road Rescue and Recovery Association (RRRA), and the Association of Vehicle Recovery Operators (AVRO), are striving to stamp out the cowboy image and introduce newer, safer working practices with the emphasis on operator training. Gone are the days of the old battered Land Rover with a length of rusty chain being used to recover vehicles of all sizes and weights. These days, modern vehicles with their expensive alloy front bumpers, plastic under bumper air dams and other bolt on goodies have dictated a fresh approach to a skill that is as old as motoring itself......vehicle recovery.

Left: Built on a new chassis, Lantern's Iveco Eurotech is fitted with a new Recoverer crane, twin winches and a hydraulic underlift. The truck was built at Worldwide Recovery Systems factory in Hertford and the bodywork was designed by Lantern and the Worldwide engineers working together.

Heavy Towing & Recovery / Field Services Atkinson
Viewline was originally a Pickfords heavy haulage tractor.
The unit, which previously saw service with BRS in the
Midlands, is powered by a Cummins 250 and fitted with a
6-speed ZF gearbox and is equipped with a RS 2000 by
Maintruck. The picture shows the righting of a Scania 112
6x2 tautliner artic after a roll-over at the Drake Circus
roundabout in Plymouth. The Atkinson is now out of
service and up for sale.

7

Above: This Matador operated by W.H. Dolman has a cab style that has remained virtually as it was when it left the factory nearly 50 years ago. A Harvey Frost crane is fitted along with bodywork that incorporates a covered work area. Modern recovery vehicle manufacturers or operators no longer favour this style of body.

Left above: Sayers' 0835 Matador was released by the M.o.D. in 1970. It was bought as a back-up vehicle to their resplendent Militant featured elsewhere. As can be seen from the photograph, its secondary role was of snow clearance for Berkshire County Council. A task it performed admirably alongside its big sister.

Left: Stylishly converted by the Burnley & Pendle Bus Company, this smart looking Matador fitted with a Harvey Frost crane, was later sold to V.J. Harper of Wisbech, a haulage contractor who occasionally used it to recover failures in his fleet. Matadors were always a favourite among bus companies and many have received quite extensive cab and body modifications sometimes utilising body panels similar to the type of bus operated.

Right: London Brick's AEC Matador is seen here at Scratchwood Services in the Autumn of 1974 assisting the company's Scammell Constructor recovery vehicle (featured elsewhere in this book) which was recovering a broken down AEC Mk V.

9

Left: An ex RAF AEC 0854 6x6 formed the basis of this fine recovery vehicle owned by Airdrie-based haulage Contractor John Hunter photographed at their yard in March 1976. Over 1500 examples were built for the RAF as fuel bowsers and a good many of these sound vehicles found employment in civilian life as heavy recovery tractors once hostilities ended.

Right: 894 FUF originally saw service with the British Army during W.W.II. After being sold off it was bought by the Maidstone & District Bus Company who fitted it with a twin boom crane. Sold out of service in the early Eighties it was bought and converted to a more traditional specification but retained the modern cab front. The crane fitted here is by Harvey Frost.

Top right: At a casual glance, most people would think that this vehicle was an old Atkinson but a closer inspection would reveal that underneath the smart coach built body this is in fact an AEC Militant. Now owned by Granthams Recovery of Spalding, the vehicle is fitted with a TFL T20 crane that has a 20-ton lifting capacity when fully retracted. Criton Engineering of Essex carried out the conversion in the late 1960s. The recovery vehicle logo behind the driver's door is that of the Association of Vehicle Recovery Operators, (A.V.R.O.) a trade association that many operators belong to.

Right: Circus King's Militant was supplied and converted in the late Seventies for Holden & Hartleys of Burnley, an East Lancs Bedford main dealer. The Ampthill-based L.W. Vass organisation, which specialises in ex-military vehicles, carried out the sale and conversion. The truck is fitted with a Harvey Frost Atlas 12 hydraulic crane and looks every inch a heavy recovery vehicle but when General Motors closed Bedford Trucks down, the dealer, like so many, lost their franchise. After standing idle for some time the truck was sold on and eventually passed into the hands of its present owner whose big top circus was visiting the Yorkshire seaside resort of Scarborough in the summer of 1993 when the photograph was taken.

Left: Many Mk V Mammoth Majors enjoyed a second career as recovery vehicles. Whites Commercials example is fitted with a Harvey Frost crane and at some time late in its life has received Bedford TK combined side light and indicator assemblies to the front corner panels.

Below far left: An AEC Mk V Mammoth Major converted from one of H Tideswell's working fleet. It was photographed at their Kingsley, Stoke-on-Trent yard in 1980. The company was a great supporter of the Southall manufacturer and a number of their early models have been restored in their fleet colours.

Left below: Designed as a recovery unit by Scammell Lorries Ltd, the Militant III featured a 5-ton slewing crane and a 15-ton main winch. It was used by the British Army as a medium recovery vehicle, having 6-wheel drive and powered by the AV760 diesel engine. This well kept example christened the 'Munchengladbach Deserter' and carrying the emblem of the Royal Electrical and Mechanical Engineers belonged to David Crouch of Leicester and was used for off-road recovery. The six slotted bars on the front bumper are ground anchors and can be linked together and pinned into the ground to form an anchorage point for winching operations. In the absence of other natural forms of anchorage such as trees and rocks, these items of equipment can prove most valuable.

Above: Sayers Transport of Newbury, Berkshire were an international road haulage company with a predominantly Scania-based fleet. Chief amongst the fleet was the 'Wessex Retriever', an AEC Militant III. Bought from the MoD, it was extensively re-furbished and kept in immaculate condition by its owners. When not being used on recovery duties it served as a yard crane and during the winter carried out snow ploughing duties for Berkshire County Council, hence the large bracket on the front bumper. The coach at the rear of the truck had just been recovered after suffering a failure on the way to an AEC Society rally.

Above: John Boardman operates depots at many of the service areas on the M6 where he provides maintenance facilities on site and a 24-hr car and commercial recovery service for that particular motorway. Amongst his large fleet of heavy recovery vehicles was this ageing AEC Mammoth Major photographed at the Hilton Park service area. Fitted with a Holmes W45 twin boom crane and a wooden body, the truck was primarily on stand-by for accident recovery. The absence of side stabilising legs limited the vehicle's side winching capacity but did not affect its lift and tow capability. It was scrapped in 1989.

Right: Based in picturesque Milnthorpe was John Douthwaite & Sons' Mammoth Major. An unusual feature of the jib is the manual extension which can be seen at the back in its travelling position. The extension is flipped over until it butts up against the main jib thus extending it by approximately 3ft. Lifting is carried out by two hydraulic rams and a 9-ton vertical spindle winch is fitted. This type of winch differs by having the rope drum mounted on its side so the rope lays from top to bottom instead of the more conventional type which has the drum vertical and lays the rope from side to side.

Below & right below: Used as a petrol tanker until 1978, Q878 PES was bought by Newtyle Commercials of Dundee where it has undergone several major transformations. The first of which was the construction of an underlift, this utilising sections of a Priestman crane and a Hymac loading shovel. The first attempt was reasonably successful but it was thought certain design changes would improve its performance so some radical surgery was performed which entailed removing the fourth axle and Hiab, constructing new bodywork and modifying the crane. Since these modifications the truck has been put back into service and has travelled extensively throughout the U.K.

Above: Newtyle's AEC Marshall Major was caught on film at the 1996 AEC Society commencing its journey back to Scotland with one of Richard Lawson's car transporters which had come to grief near the Dartford Tunnel in London.

As can be seen, the cab has received quite a substantial sleeping compartment and the vehicle sports a Buffalo front grille. The crane is loosely designed along the lines of the TFL T20.

Above: Frank Ratcliffe and Son owned and operated AECs from their Peterborough base for many years. Amongst them was WFL 68H, a Mammoth Major equipped with a Mk2 Interstater underlift and a Gar-Wood winch. The fitting of modern equipment to an elderly truck shows the great affinity and trust that the Ratcliffes placed in this particular breed of vehicle. An Atlas crane adds to the recovery capabilities and the controls can be seen in the vertical position alongside the winch.

Above right: Originally operated by C.D. Bramall of Leeds and powered by the AV760 engine, Buffgate Motors Ergomatic-cabbed Mammoth Major Six has the TFL T12 hydraulic crane and an all-steel body. The chassis is a heavy-duty tipper model.

Right: Photographed in September 1980, the AEC based eight wheeler belonging to Buckdale was equipped with a TFL T20 crane. It was seen at the Elston storage depot near Bedford. Worthy of note are the twin lens reflex mirrors which were popular in the Seventies due to their providing a standard and a wide angle view to the rear.

Left: This AEC badged vehicle was operated by Troopers Lodge Garage, Blockley, the picture dating from August 1978. Although carrying AEC badges and front grill, the fuel tank and rear axles are of Leyland origin, suggesting that the vehicle may have been recabbed at some time in its life. Recovery gear is by Gar-Wood and is the type fitted to the M1 and M1A1 class of wartime recovery vehicle built by Kenworth and Ward Le France. The wheelbase on this vehicle must have made manoeuvring in tight spaces extremely difficult.

Below left: Looking more akin to railway engineering than road rescue is Quenchport of Burnley's AEC which is fitted with a much-modified Coles crane. The girder type jib has a hydraulic extension but raising and lowering is carried out by steel cables. The power-take-off (p.t.o.) is driven through the main gearbox and an unusual safety feature is the brake chamber fitted on the front bumper next to the offside headlamp. This is connected to the clutch pedal and in the event of an emergency, a switch is thrown which operates the chamber, thus pressing the clutch pedal and disengaging the drive to the p.t.o. which in turn brings everything to a halt until the switch is reversed and the drive re-engaged. When last seen in January 1993 the truck was undergoing a major rebuild.

Right: This short wheelbase Albion Caledonian equipped with the twin-boom Holmes 750 was being operated by Wincanton Garages of Helston in June 1975. The cut-down eight wheeler's origins might well have been in serving in Wincanton Transport's fleet of Caledonian tankers.

Left: AEC trucks and Harvey Frost cranes have been linked together since civilian operators started fitting them on ex military Matador chassis. This more modern pairing features an Ergomatic-cabbed Mandator chassis in the livery of Fleur-De-Lys-Pies Ltd of Warwick. Used primarily for the recovery of a fleet of delivery vehicles, it is powered by an example of the ill-fated V8 800 Series engine that suffered from reliability problems which resulted in it being withdrawn from production after only three years.

Left and far left: A brace of immaculate Atkinsons here, both owned by Johnsons of Banks near Southport. The swb example was first operated by British Road Services and is from a batch fitted with the AEC 470 engine. The lwb version has a Cummins diesel engine and features an underlift designed and built in Johnson's own workshops. Like all of their vehicles, the Atkinsons were kept in tip-top condition with the underlift once being the recipient of a trophy for being the best kept working recovery vehicle.

Left: B. Barnes of Rawtenstall in Lancashire operates a large fleet of Seddon Atkinson rigids on national haulage. Any failures in the fleet are retrieved by their Atkinson recovery vehicle, photographed here rescuing a Leyland Roadrunner that had come to grief entering a motorway slip road. The lifting equipment consists of a 5-ton hydraulic jib, which can be extended manually by means of a cranking handle, but a more conventional rigid tow bar was the favoured means of recovery on this occasion.

Right: Killingbeck Transport of Blackburn operated many Atkinsons in their haulage fleet and still holds a great affinity for the marque. Still earning its keep in the 1990s is their Gardner 240-powered recovery vehicle converted from a 1975 Borderer tractor unit. The frame attached to the front bumper is the mast off a forklift truck thus enabling the vehicle to be used for the loading and unloading of goods in its owner's yard.

Above: Ryland's impressive Atkinson eight wheeler used to operate out of their Walton Summit base, close to the M6 motorway at Preston during the time the company held the Seddon Atkinson franchise. Built from a chassis cab, the Cummins powered vehicle was fitted with a Holmes 750 crane with hydraulic extending booms. When the company name and franchise changed to Lancashire Leyland Daf, the Ryland name was unceremoniously covered with decals advertising this fact and shortly afterwards the vehicle passed into the JDS Group who in turn sold the vehicle on.

Right: WGC 625G started life as a heavy haulage unit with Pickfords, (Trucks in Britain Pickfords p44). Built with the Viewline cab, it was owned by Bridge Mill service station of Edenfield, Lancs. After suffering a broken windscreen the owners experienced great difficulty in obtaining a replacement so it was decided that a cab off one of Holt Lane Transport's eight wheelers would be fitted. Problems arose when, after fitment of the cab, it was discovered that the front axle was set slightly further forward so surgery was performed on the wheel arches and lower portions of the cab front panel, hence the slight misshape around the front wheels. The truck was later sold to Wignalls and fitted with a manual underlift.

Below and below right: Once operated by BRS Rescue, Newtyles Viewline was given a new lease of life in their Dundee workshop where a total refurbishment was carried out. The original TFL T20 crane was overhauled and an underlift designed and built to compliment it. The actual lifting is still carried out by the T20 but the underlift gives damage-free recovery capabilities. However, the short wheelbase does limit its lift and tow capacity.

Left and left below: Mick Gould's Autocar came into this country from South Africa where it had been used as a dumper. Peter and David Cosby, who are based at Kirton Holme, near Boston, Lincs, set about removing the tipping body, and fitted the 8 ton Coles slewing crane with two 10 ton winches, before selling it to the East Sussex operator who runs a fleet of customised American trucks. Christened 'The Ugly Dog', the most prominent features are the long bonnet which hides the Caterpillar engine, and the position of the headlamps which are mounted just ahead of the front wheels.

Below: Developed in the 1950s from the Bedford S type, the RL was produced in large numbers and in many guises. The version shown here is powered by a Vauxhall 6-cylinder petrol engine that transmitted the drive to the front axle via a two-speed transfer box. The recovery equipment consists of a chassis mounted 10 ton Boughton winch which is driven off the main gearbox, and a Gar-Wood twin boom crane fitted with dual controls. Compare the boom design of the Gar-Wood with that of the Holmes cranes - totally different in design, but yet the principal of operation remains the same.

Above: AWD's attempt to enter the lucrative tank transporter market culminated in this prototype being built, albeit now seen in recovery guise. Powered by a 400 hp Cummins engine, the AWD has six wheel drive and is over three metres wide. The cab is the Bedford TM version being modified to provide a flat floor. The Brimec recovery equipment and body was fitted by Roger Dysons and the truck can be regularly seen working on the roads of the north east of England.

Above: The Lancashire-based meat pie manufacturer Walter Holland & Sons are famous for the care they take over their large fleet of delivery vans. Because of this, the vehicles become much sought after on the second hand market. Nook Lane Garage purchased their J type in 1983 when it was released from Holland's fleet. They proceeded to add a 3-ton capacity hydraulic boom and a small rotating crane capable of handling damaged motor cycles. Even with a change of owner, the truck was still kept in exceptional condition.

Top left: Built in 1965 and formerly with the M.o.D., T & G Fox's diesel-powered R type was converted into a recovery vehicle when the company was involved in road haulage operations. During a lean spell, they diversified into horticulture and the Bedford was kept on to look after the remaining vehicles. Now sporting a TK front bumper and kept in immaculate condition it is hard to believe that, when photographed, this was still a working truck.

Left: Twin boom cranes come in various weight capacities. Shown here on Briggs Bedford M type is a Bulldog 10 crane manufactured by Wreckers International. Fitted with twin 5-ton winches, one of the main differences between this and other models of twin boom cranes is the use of links instead of the more traditional steel cables to support the main lifting booms. The links are adjustable to allow the height of the booms to be altered.

Above: Two stroke diesels have never been popular in British road going vehicles. Examples like the Rootes TS3 and the Foden two-stroke came and went with operators favouring the more traditional four stroke engines. Wards Bedford TM 4400 however, was fitted with a Silver 96 Series V6 Detroit Diesel coupled to a Fuller 9-speed gearbox. Built in 1983 for Brighton Recovery by Wreckers International, it featured a Mk 1 Interstater underlift, a 10t dp winch and hydraulic rear spades. The combination of a high revving engine and a relatively high overall gearing gave this truck an acceleration that would not disgrace some family saloons. Sadly an engine failure saw the Detroit ousted in favour of a Cummins power plant. The photograph shows a Mercedes 1114 that was 'torched' outside its owner's premises and was on its way for disposal due to the severity of the damage caused.

Above: Critchleys of Burscough operate a varied fleet of recovery vehicles. Amongst which, is this Cummins-powered short wheelbase Bedford TM fitted with Bulldog twin boom equipment. It was photographed collecting a Ford Cargo which had been involved in an accident.

Above: XPG 861T is a 1979 model Bedford TK operated in the colours of the Motorway Rescue Services. Photographed at their Charnock Richard depot, the truck is fitted with a Holmes 480 crane and a spec lift. The 480 is the smallest of the Holmes twin booms and is designed primarily for light vehicle recovery, and as such it has no side stabilisers. The bodywork is by Crane Fruehauf, the trailer manufacturers, who were Holmes concessionaires for a short while in the early Eighties.

Above right: Baker Redhill, a General Motors main dealer, asked Roger Dyson Recovery Systems to build them an Enforcer underlift on a Bedford TL chassis. The stylish bodywork incorporates roller shutter doors on the equipment lockers and the truck was seen at the 1985 A.V.R.O show which was held at Warwick that year.

Right: A long-term fan of the Bedford marque is Jon Beech of Stoke-on-Trent who has operated several different models within his fleet. Seen here is one of a pair of TMs fitted with ACB lifting gear. The truck was driven by 'Lofty' Ailwood who regularly travelled the length and breadth of the country in the Cummins-powered variant.

Above: Syd Abrams of Manchester had this much modified TM fitted with a Ty-Rite LG10 heavy lift system for damage free recovery. An eye-catching truck, the cab was extended by fitting additional side panels behind the cab doors. The raised roof, apart from creating an aerodynamic look, gives almost 6 feet of standing room in the cab; the beacon being some 13ft from the ground. Powered by a V8 Detroit Diesel, the truck was disposed of in 1992, it was later acquired by the Crooklands Motor Company near Kendal.

Above left: Walkden Commercials designed and built their own spec lift in their Farnworth workshops. Built on a TL 1830 tractor unit, the spec lift has a 1.5 ton lift and tow capacity. Having a g.t.w. of 18 tons, the truck is capable of rigid-bar towing larger commercials of up to approximately 14 tons in weight, providing the vehicle being towed has adequate brakes and a competent steersman.

Left: Presentation and image have gained an importance over the past few years and BOC Transhield were very aware of public image when they commissioned this Bedford TM 6x4 with TFL T20 equipment. Based at the company's Faversham depot, it sports a body built of chequer plate and a roof mounted air conditioning unit.

Above: There is nothing worse than a vehicle disgracing itself in front of a large crowd. When the monster truck 'Rocket' did just such a thing at the 1995 Scottish Truckfest, it was left to Kerr & Smith's Enforcer equipped 6x6 TM to save the day by recovering the stricken Chevrolet from the arena.

Above: Steve Young's originally built this slewing crane for Unity Garage of Leicester and mounted it on a 4x2 AEC Mandator. The crane and Darlington winch performed admirably for many years and through several changes of ownership until it was decided that the equipment would be better suited fitted to a larger capacity chassis. Subsequently the entire crane, winch and bodywork was transplanted on to this Daf 2800 6x4 christened 'The Pig'. The truck was operated by Salthouse Commercials and later passed on to Powells Garages of Cardiff.

Top left: Built in 1942, Jobson's CMP Chevrolet C605 saw extensive service during World War II with the Canadian Armed Forces. In 1993 when over fifty years old, the petrol engined 4x4 was still going strong, being a regular sight in and around the Bolton area. Bought from a dealer in 1974, the Gar-Wood equipped truck evaded several attempts by its owner to restore it as often duty called and off she would go on yet another in a long list of recovery jobs.

Left above: Century Motors of Farnworth near Bolton operated two of these 4x4 GMC Chevy Blazer pick-ups. Both were fitted with a fixed jib, lifting slings and Warn electric winches. EHD 730V was the newer of the two and has passenger accommodation behind the driver. It is seen here with a sight that has become all too familiar in these seemingly lawless times; the remains of a stolen Fiesta XR2, severely damaged and minus its wheels and several other items of original equipment.

Left: Dafs have always been a popular chassis on which to base a recovery unit. Albany Recovery Services are based near to Birmingham's notorious 'Spaghetti Junction' and this is their Daf 2300 which was fitted with an E.K.A. underlift and an Atlas crane. The body style is of the curvilinear type, incorporating plenty of locker storage space for all the ancillary equipment required when dealing with stricken vehicles.

Above: Lamb Hill's 3300 has a Liberator underlift built by MSM Engineering of Kirkaldy in Scotland. Seen here towing a Bedford with a seized engine, the truck had actually passed out of Devon-based Lamb Hill's ownership and was being used as a courtesy loan vehicle by the Roger Dyson Group when photographed in June 1993. An interesting design feature of the MSM bodywork is the amount of room available inside the lockers where virtually the whole of the upper section is dedicated to equipment storage. The vehicle now operates in the fleet of IGW of Bolton.

Above: 'Thunderbird 6' is MV Recovery's left-hand-drive Daf 3300 with Concept recovery equipment by Wreckers International. This consists of an extending boom beneath which is fitted the underlift. The winch cables are fed through the boom head allowing the truck to become in effect a fixed crane, now a very popular configuration on modern recovery vehicles. A 'party trick' of the vehicle is shown as it, and a similarly equipped truck, carry out a full lift on a 40ft trailer.

Right: Auty Lifts of Dewsbury were a small engineering company specialising in the building of high quality recovery vehicles individually tailored to the customer's own requirements. Teales Daf 2800 has a 10t underlift fitted with a triple extension on the bottom arm giving an overall lift and reach of 4 tons at 9 feet. This is particularly useful when handling buses and coaches, which by nature of their design have the suspension units and running gear located several feet back from the extremities of their bodywork, thus requiring the long reach so that lifts may be performed damage free.

Right below: An unusual, if not unique, truck is this day cabbed DAF 3300 from the fleet of S & H. It is an 8x2 with the centre rear axle being the drive axle. The crane is separate from the underlift and can be used independently. The walk-in body houses the main recovery equipment and a cab top sleeper has been added.

Below: A & S Recovery operate this Daf from their Luton, Bedfordshire base. Fitted with a Wreckmaster twin boom, an additional feature is an underlift built by R.S. Recovery Systems which compliments the versatility of the twin boom by permitting damage free towing. Many operators with these types of cranes are fitting underlifts now to increase their vehicles versatility and earning power.

Above: Diamond T tractors formed the mainstay of many heavy recovery companies when they were released from military service after the war. Some operators still employ them in their fleet as back-up vehicles or heavy winch tractors for which the Gar-Wood winch mounted behind the cab has proved itself time after time. Coopers of Hurley's Diamond T wrecker, at rest at Toddington Services, M1 motorway on August 5th 1978, features a somewhat rudimentary closed cab, being originally built as an open cabbed example sometime after 1943. The recovery equipment is by Harvey Frost.

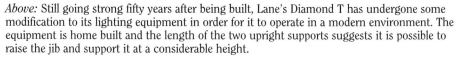

Above: Still going strong fifty years after being built, Lane's Diamond T has undergone some modification to its lighting equipment in order for it to operate in a modern environment. The equipment is home built and the length of the two upright supports suggests it is possible to raise the jib and support it at a considerable height.

Top right: Seen in the Dumfries yard of Gateside Commercials, this 230 Cummins powered Diamond Reo was built by Wreckers International and put to work as a demonstrator. Fitted with a Wreckmaster 30 crane, it travelled throughout Europe before coming back to Wreckers' Hertford base. It was from here that Gateside Commercials purchased it for specialist plant recovery, a task it performed well under the direction of workshop foreman Bob Bell. When plant recovery started to diminish, the truck was sold on to an operator in the Buxton area.

Right upper: Sawfords of Maidenhead's Diamond T 981 is an early example of the firm's preference for the U.S. built product. Note the non standard headlamps and indicators. The recovery equipment is the ever present Holmes W45.

Right: What must be the ultimate insult is the fitting of a Ford Transit cab on this Lancashire County Council Diamond T. The truck also features a Rolls Royce diesel engine in place of the original Hercules diesel. The recovery gear consists of a fixed gantry with a pulley block at one end. To achieve a lift, the winch rope is run out, fed over the pulley block and secured to the casualty. The rope is then taken in and the casualty lifted. Judging by the bend in the gantry, some very heavy lifts have been achieved this way. It was withdrawn from service in 1994.

Above: Still in remarkably good condition, and still giving good service, is this Bulldog 10 equipped 'K' Series Dodge owned by George Mutch. The 'K' Series was the forerunner to the popular Commando range of trucks that first appeared in the early Seventies.

Above left: The Dodge 50 Series was a popular choice for a light recovery vehicle. The range of gross weights from 3.5 to 7.5 tons gave them ample capacity when towing cars and light commercials. Fountain Garage's example is an S36 which is the lightest in the range and only has single wheels fitted on the rear axle. The spec lift was removed from an 'angled cab' BMC and has the hydraulics powered by an electric motor. This is a common method used on small vehicles as it does away with the need to fit expensive gearbox mounted power-take-off pumps.

Left upper: Fresh out of service with the RAC but still wearing its reflective side flash is D178 NJW, a 50 Series fitted with a Brimec 1500kg spec lift and 5 passenger accommodation. Typical of the type used by the motoring clubs, this vehicle was bought by national car auctions for collecting and delivering cars and light vans from their Haydock site. The 50 Series has now been phased out by the clubs in favour of more modern vehicles such as the Iveco 49-10.

Left: As operators of a large and varied Dodge fleet, it made good sense that when looking for a suitable chassis for their recovery vehicle, Pendle Borough Council should stay with a make they were familiar with. The resulting purchase was this ex BRS Truck Rental Commando G16 which was bought from CGL Trucks of Manchester. Roger Dyson fitted the Invader 10 hydraulic crane previously on an International Loadstar used in his works fleet. A fully skirted steel body was added along with an 8-ton winch. The truck's primary function is the recovery of local authority vehicles and it entered service in 1984 with a scheduled life span of 10 years.

Above: This 2KV cabbed 'chinese six' ERF was operated by Tunstall, Staffs. based operator A. Brown (Beaumont Garage) Ltd., part of the AB Group. It is seen at a Midlands motorway services having come to the aid of one of the company's ERFs. The recovery equipment appears to be a rudimentary in-house construction.

Above: When the time came to replace their aged Leyland Buffalo, Blackburn Transport purchased this Cummins-powered ERF to recover any failures in the Corporation bus fleet. Although fitted with lifting equipment, it is totally unsuitable for carrying out suspended tows on the more modern and fragile buses in service today. This apart, because it has the means to lift and tow a vehicle, it falls within the definition of a recovery vehicle and as such is subject to a concessionary vehicle excise duty.

Above left: Over 20 years old and still looking remarkably tidy is this LV-cabbed ERF. Fitted with basic hydraulic lifting gear, it epitomises the type of recovery vehicle used by many haulage fleets for in-house towing.

Left: This 1971 Cummins powered ERF 6x4 is owned by A.J.A. Smith, a Clitheroe-based haulier and ERF service dealer. Fitted with a Holmes 750 and a Hiab crane, this vehicle was once owned by TGB Motors who were a well-established ERF dealer before their demise in the Eighties. The truck itself was kept on hand for breakdowns within its owner's fleet and was also on call for the local police forces accident rota which covered the notorious A59 Lancashire to Yorkshire trunk road. Now retired, it is parked under a sheet in its owner's yard awaiting a major overhaul.

Above: Built in 1972 with a full sleeper cab, this LV-cabbed ERF wrecker was operated as a long wheelbase Cummins-powered rigid in the Eaton Transmissions fleet. It is thought to have been used as mobile test bed as it operated throughout its entire life with the company under trade plates. When Commercial Fleet Services bought it, they shortened the chassis, fitted a Harvey Frost crane and added the bodywork. Because it had never been registered from new, it was given a 'Q' prefix. This is awarded to those vehicles with no original registration number, vehicles imported from abroad or vehicles which have lost their original documentation or identity.

Above: Tony Sales of Rushden, Northants operated this ERF recovery vehicle equipped with Holmes recovery equipment. It is seen here in September 1988 about to recover a vintage Leyland Octopus. Note the ERF has the M Series cab which can be distinguished by the fact that the headlamps are mounted in the bumper instead of above as in the B Series cabs.

Right: Built for the Milk Marketing Board by TFL, this ERF served at the Board's Clitheroe workshops until their close in the late Eighties. It transferred to the Bamber Bridge workshops of MD Foods under re-organisation of the business and was then redeployed when that workshop closed in the mid Nineties. The body style is basic but functional, all the equipment being stored on the open back.

Right: It took Steve Jarnell of B&S Recovery over two years to complete his recovery vehicle - work could only be carried out when the truck was standing idle. The chassis is an ex Fine Fare tractor unit being powered by a Rolls Eagle diesel. The underlift was bought in kit form and assembled by the staff at B&S who also extended the chassis, added an extending boom and built the all steel bodywork.

Right below: Just like Walsh & Dearden's recovery vehicle overleaf, Green Brothers ERF is one of a pair, also used in connection with a vehicle dismantling business. Although much shorter and very manoeuvrable, this truck is also kept in good condition. Fitted with an Auty Lifts custom-built crane, the truck is painted a striking lime green colour. An interesting feature of the crane is that instead of having an extending boom, the entire drop arm extends to allow precise coupling up to be achieved.

Left: Walsh & Dearden's E14 is part of a fleet of vehicles used in connection with the owner's vehicle dismantling and haulage companies. Built at their East Lancs. depot, the truck is kept in tip-top condition and helps present a modern efficient image far removed from people's perceptions of 'scrap yard' recovery vehicles.

Below left: Mason & Darlow's 6x4 is fitted with a Holmes 750 crane and a Crane Fruehauf body. Worthy of note is the fact that the booms for a 6 or 8-wheeled chassis are some 20 inches longer than those fitted to a 4-wheeled chassis. This is to allow the mast to be set further forward, thus avoiding fouling of the foremost drive axle by any part of the crane but still allowing the ropes to fall clear of the tailgate.

Below: When Kevin Shanley was looking for a recovery vehicle to compliment his truck repair business he decided to have a go and build his own. The first job was to refurbish the ERF chassis and replace the trusty Gardner engine with a 320 Cummins. He then set about building the underlift crane and body to his own exacting requirements. The resulting vehicle is a very creditable first attempt and the truck has made several trips across the water to rescue stranded vehicles in mainland Europe.

Above: Seen making sedate progress along Blackpool Promenade with a Krupp 4x4 mobile crane in tow is John Marsh's 6x4 ERF. The vehicle actually started life as a 30ft rigid but in 1987 it was converted to a recovery vehicle to a design drawn up by BVT's engineering staff. Power comes from a 320 Rolls diesel and the truck has a gross train weight of 56 tons. The recovery crane is a Brimec Centurion underlift of 15 tons capacity and a Ramsey hydraulic winch is fitted. Entering service with BVT in 1988, the truck replaced an ageing Atkinson 6-wheeler.

Above: Castle Cement's recovery vehicle carries a Holmes 750 crane transferred from an LV cabbed eight wheeler which served the Clitheroe based company for many years. Seen here delivering a Renault R340 to JDS Trucks at Blackburn for a clutch repair, the body modification to accept the vehicle's second axle can be seen. Castle Cement was known as Ribble Cement for many years.

Above left: Richard Read's spectacular recovery unit started life as a day-cabbed 3-axle heavy haulage tractor unit. Reads purchased it and fitted it with the recovery equipment from an ex army Leyland Martian. It was in this guise that the truck operated for several years before undergoing a major transformation. The chassis was extended, a fourth lifting axle was fitted and an extended sleeper cab fabricated and fitted to create this truly individual truck.

Left: When Steadplans ageing ERF was retired from front line service, it was stripped of its equipment and put out to grass. Meanwhile this E14 8x4 was sent to Les Wallings where he refurbished the twin boom and Hiab, built a new body and fitted a Boniface Mk2E Interstater crane on it. Wallings also fitted a Darlington winch behind the 750 mast.

Right: Still surviving after nearly 50 years is Bassetts Roadways' 'Hercules'. The vehicle commenced life in 1940 as a Foden DG6/10 being supplied to the RAF where it was later fitted with a crane and replacement 6LW engine. Originally acquired for spare parts only, the chassis was totally rebuilt as a heavy duty recovery vehicle, the conversion work all being undertaken in the company's workshops. It underwent a further rebuild in the 1970's incorporating such items as a Gardner 6LX engine, 12-speed gearbox air brakes, power steering and revised bodywork incorporating a new windscreen. The vehicle has now been retired.

Above: Originally built as a tipper, B&S Haulage acquired their Foden eight-wheeler when it was put out to grass after the regular driver retired. Steve Jarnell then set about the task of designing and building the lifting gear in his friend's farmyard. After giving many years service the Foden passed on into the hands of a vehicle dismantler who cut the chassis and exported the Gardner 150 engine to power a junk on the South China Seas.

Right: Doncaster in November 1975 is the setting for this N.C.B. FG fitted with an S18 cab and Harvey Frost gear. When photographed, the Foden was about to tow start the Bedford gulley emptier, hence the chain attached to the TK's front towing eye.

Below right: James Street Motors of Bury specialise in providing recovery facilities for roadwork contra-flow sections on many of Britain's busiest motorways. The fleet was predominantly Foden and their yard is an absolute delight for fans of the marque as it contains many examples, some of which are still in use. Fleet no. 1 was a Gardner powered S21, it having a hydraulic extending jib surrounded by a basic but functional body. The truck was disposed of in the early Nineties and was seen in Frank Owen's yard before being broken up for spares.

Below: This exceptionally well kept example is operated by a Foden service dealer in the manufacturer's home town. Finished in chocolate brown and cream, the truck has a Harvey Frost crane and sports a traditional wooden body but has gained along the way some larger than life mirror arms.

Above: Normans of Manchester operated their S20 cabbed Foden for many years before being absorbed into the Greenline group of companies. Fitted with a Harvey Frost crane and a coachbuilt body, the truck was stolen by joyriders who rammed a building and then abandoned it in a ditch. The cab was so badly damaged the vehicle was towed into storage in the hope that a new cab could be found. Seen here on its way courtesy of Ward's Mercedes, the truck was later sold for preservation.

Above left: Thomas Fox's S20 cabbed Foden was an airport fuel tanker before being converted for towing duties and was powered by a much-modified Gardner 180 diesel engine. The tow bar that is mounted on the side of the body is called a 'swan neck' and is shaped to enable it to be fitted directly onto the casualty's front axle by means of a special clamp. This type of bar is very useful for towing heavy vehicles where the manufacturers towing eye is inadequate or where there is no towing facility available at all.

Left: In the Somercotes yard of Cotes Park Commercials Ltd, could be found a wide variety of Foden vehicles, which were maintained by the Derby-based company. Amongst them was their very own S39 cabbed 8-wheeler fitted with a Holmes W45 crane and a Darlington winch mounted behind the cab. As well as providing recovery facilities for its own customers, the truck was regularly seen recovering accident-damaged vehicles on behalf of the local and county constabularies.

Recovery vehicles can be as complicated or as simple as an operator requires. Timmins' Foden S41 carries the most basic of recovery cranes namely a moveable girder type jib with a hook at the end. This satisfied the operator's need at the time but would be unacceptable with modern vehicles and safety practices in today's market place.

Above: The twin boom crane is a versatile piece of kit but even this has its limitations, so Burrows of Borrowash specified this accident unit which includes a 6-ton HMF slewing crane. The crane extends to over 30 feet and towers above the 750 installation. To stabilise the truck during lifting operations, two sets of hydraulic legs are fitted. One pair at the crane's base and one pair tucked in between the rear wheels.

Above left: Simpson's Foden was formerly a tractor unit with Whitbread Brewery until local used vehicle dealer F. Dugdale & Sons of Nelson, Lancs. purchased it. Dugdales set about extending the chassis before Simpsons fitted a Holmes W45 crane which had been removed from an elderly Diamond T 969 and put the vehicle to work. Laid up in 1989 due to a change in company policy, the Foden was sold on to a local haulage contractor who used it to recover vehicles for his own fleet and repair business.

Left: With a Yorkshire registration but working out of their Torquay depot, this Foden S40 operated in the large fleet of Leeds-based coach operator Wallace Arnold. Fitted with Holmes W45 recovery gear and a special towing hitch to facilitate the recovery of coaches in its care, the vehicle served well into the Eighties when it was withdrawn and scrapped. The absence of large hub reduction units suggest this vehicle may have started life as a rigid chassis rather than a heavy haulage tractor unit.

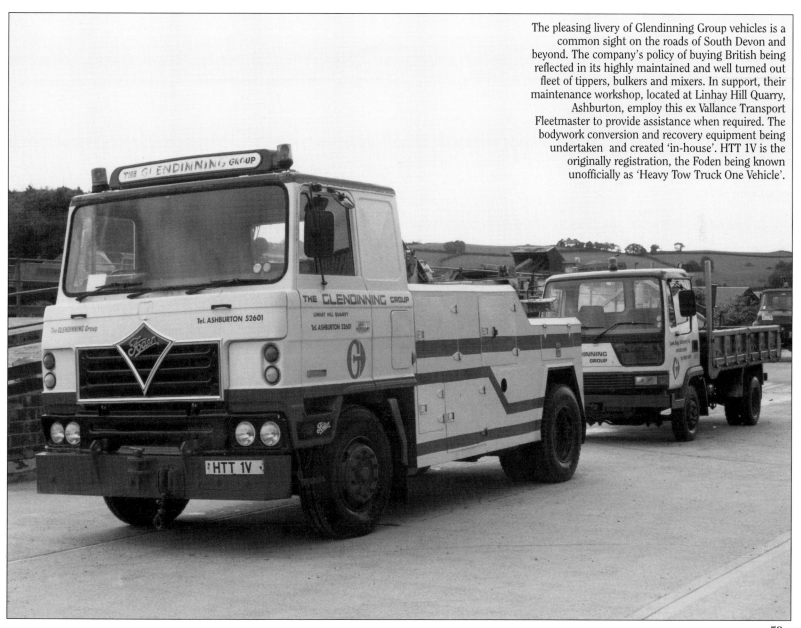

The pleasing livery of Glendinning Group vehicles is a common sight on the roads of South Devon and beyond. The company's policy of buying British being reflected in its highly maintained and well turned out fleet of tippers, bulkers and mixers. In support, their maintenance workshop, located at Linhay Hill Quarry, Ashburton, employ this ex Vallance Transport Fleetmaster to provide assistance when required. The bodywork conversion and recovery equipment being undertaken and created 'in-house'. HTT 1V is the originally registration, the Foden being known unofficially as 'Heavy Tow Truck One Vehicle'.

Eight wheelers were never very popular in the past as recovery vehicles due to their being so cumbersome and difficult to manoeuvre. Recently many operators have changed their attitude towards them because of their ability to lift and tow loaded casualties without overloading their own rear axles or suffering steering loss. Egerton's Foden was one such example of the modern breed, being fitted with an Interstater underlift and a 10-ton dp winch.

Above: The City of Bristol Transport Services operated this S80 model fitted with a Cummins 355 engine and having a train weight of 100 tons. The crane is a Bulldog 30 which is of a similar pattern to a Holmes 750. Fitted with off-road tyres on the rear bogie, the axles feature hub reduction gearing which is deployed by turning a collar on the outer hub casing. This allows extra heavy loads to be moved without damaging the drive-line.

Above right: This Foden belonging to Wards of Leeds was once an eight wheeled bulk powder tanker. Wards removed both rear axles, shortened the chassis and fitted a tractor unit drive axle. The underlift is a TFL 'T' lift and the ERF being recovered had suffered the indignation of a broken prop shaft.

Right: When Les Walling of Broughton near Preston designed and built his recovery unit there were two main features that set it apart. The first was the length of the bottom arm fitted to the underlift. This was built especially long to cope with the recovery of buses and coaches, a field in which Wallings specialise. The second was that the entire recovery crane was built on a demountable subframe, which could be removed, and a flat platform installed in its place, thus allowing goods to be loaded with the 15-ton Effer crane. Although novel in its conception, the design was later changed and a full curvilinear body was permanently fitted along with a modified underlift.

Above: Prior to the acceptance of the current Foden recovery tractor, a small number of gun tractor chassis were purchased and adapted to fit the EKA crane and bodywork similar to the Scammell Crusader already in military service. However, R.E.M.E. required a vehicle that was multi-purpose and capable for use as a crane, so this model was dropped in favour of its larger and more versatile stablemate. This example, one of three sold at auction in 1992, was still wearing its black and green colour scheme when photographed later. David Crouch later purchased one as did J. & A. Recovery.

Above left: All Recovery & Repair of Guildford have operated Fodens for many years. Their 6x6 shown here was designed and built by Syren and was at the time reputed to be the most powerful winch truck in the U.K. It was built primarily for the recovery of heavy items of plant and machinery, the inclusion of a heavy duty underlift meant that it can be used to recover 'on highway' vehicles also. The two massive hydraulic rear spades are used to anchor the truck when performing heavy winch operations. The winch mounted on the front bumper is of 10 tons capacity and can be used for self-recovery. Built on an ex military chassis and weighing over 20 tons, the truck entered service in 1989.

Left: Another example of the adapted Foden gun tractor chassis. Now bearing a civilian registration and working for the Birmingham Coach Company, it is seen rendering assistance to a failed National Express double-deck coach. Inside the open lock appears to be a large concrete block. This is to provide ballast for lifting and towing.

Above: Photographed in August 1995 is an example of the Foden Medium Mobility 6x6 recovery vehicle issued to the British Army in the late Eighties/ early Nineties. This example was based at Ward Barracks, Bulford, home of 414 Troop, Tank Transporter Regiment where it provided vital support to the REME workshops responsible for the maintenance of the large fleet of Scammell Commanders and Crusaders based there.

Above left: Developed for H.M. Forces as a medium mobility, go anywhere, do anything recovery vehicle, the Foden's directive was to recover all types of military wheeled vehicles from whatever terrain they might be located. Powered by the Perkins Eagle diesel coupled to a Fuller gearbox and Kirkstall axles, the recovery equipment consists of a 12 ton Atlas slewing crane, an EKA underlift for suspended towing, a 25 ton main winch and a 10 ton self-recovery winch mounted at the front. An order of 333 of these vehicles was placed for the British Army, some being issued to T.A. units.

Above and left: One that got away. One of four Foden Medium Mobility recovery vehicles built for the evolution and development programme in 1984 prior to production examples being ordered by the M.o.D. A further 22 have since been ordered as replacements for losses through attrition. Released in 1991, it was purchased by Jim Frodsham of Frodsham Motors who operates it out of his Morcombelake, Dorset premises on specialist recovery work in the South West.

Right: Photographed at the 1997 RN & BAEE Farnborough, September 1997 was this Foden Ekalift 2500 Recovery Unit. The Ekalift 2500 is mounted on the Foden British Army improved Medium Mobility Load Carrier chassis, its recovery device having a maximum lift capacity of 12 tonnes enabling the heaviest of the Army's wheeled transport to be handled. The vehicle also features a supplementary extending boom for smaller vehicles and incorporates a capstan winch with constant line speed with a 25 tonne line pull over the entire length. It is also equipped with a 12.5 tonne or 25 metre-tonne crane to assist in the recovery task or workshop duties.

TFL of Bedfordshire produced two models of single boom cranes, the T750 and the larger T12 as shown here. With a capacity of 12 tons closed and 4 tons fully extended, it has a simple two-lever operation making it easy to use. Tom Mellors of Rochdale had many years trouble free service from their T12 which was fitted to a 6-wheel D Series chassis along with a TFL designed all-steel body, seen here minus the battery access flap.

Above: After standing idle for some years, E&D Commercials D Series was sold to a garage in Todmorden near Halifax where the crane was refurbished and fitted to a newer chassis. Formerly owned by the Skipper Motor Group, the crane was lifted by two hydraulic rams and had a jib extension powered out by an internal ram.

Above right: Apart from performing the run of the mill lift and tow recoveries, 'Rambo', D. & A.J. Heaton's spec lift equipped D Series, had the honour of towing their restored Humber reconnaissance vehicle believed to be one of only two surviving examples in existence. Attending various rallies and events in the summer makes a welcome change from the truck's everyday tasks.

Right middle : Miller's D Series was assembled in their Longton Workshop near Preston. Powered by a Perkins V8 diesel, it was fitted with a Davewell Engineering underlift incorporating a hydraulic extension in the top boom thus converting the vehicle into a static crane, a useful option when used on accident recovery. The truck is now owned and operated by F. Audsley & Sons of Southport.

Right: For many years the Ford Transit has been a popular choice for light vehicle recovery but recently operators and police forces have been concerned about the possibility of exceeding the rear axle capacity when towing large cars and vans. One solution is to opt for a larger vehicle such as the Iveco Daily, another is to uprate the axle capacity of the Transit in some way. Faced with this problem, L.T.R. of Stoke-on-Trent built their 6 wheeler Transit by adding a self-steering axle behind the original drive axle. The staff, who design and build their own recovery units, also designed and built the bodywork, the spec lift and modified the panel work to incorporate a crew cab for passenger accommodation.

Above: Another member of the Cheshire based Egerton fleet was Q586 GJA, a Ford 0609 A Series. Referred to by the manufacturer as the 'go between', the A Series breached the gap between the largest Transit and the smallest D Series. Egerton's version has a crew cab for the passengers and a Holmes Commander hydraulic crane equipped with twin winches. For damage free towing, a Holmes spec lift is fitted and when not in use it is stored on the vehicle deck underneath the crane.

Above left: Built by Reynolds Boughton in the early Eighties, J&S' spec lift equipped vehicle has four wheel drive capability. Because the vehicle stands higher than a standard A Series, the headlamps have been lowered to bring them within the limits required by the Construction and Use regulations. An interesting point is the difference in size between the front and rear tyres.

Left: The Ford Transcontinental was always an impressive vehicle and the tall Berliet designed cab gave a commanding presence. Many entered recovery fleets and gave sterling service as did Allways Garages Holmes equipped example. The two upright levers at the back are for operating the twin winches independently.

Above: Perry's Transcontinental is a big truck in every way. From the large front bumper to the crane at the rear, everything about this vehicle is big. Stored in the box behind the cab are a set of air cushions and a vast array of ancillary equipment. The crane has an 11 ton lifting capacity and there are two Gar-Wood winches, one either side of the crane base. Large recovery trucks like this are ideally suited to motorway work because their size can prove a handful when negotiating towns and cities whilst towing another vehicle. A company support vehicle is parked alongside.

Above: As with other types of specialist bodywork, recovery cranes outlive the chassis life and are transferred onto a newer chassis. The underlift on Wards Mercedes was already on its second life when it was refurbished and again transferred onto a more modern chassis. The remains of the Mercedes were sold to David Crouch of Leicester who collected it on this Brimec equipped Cargo and as can be seen, removal of the crane necessitated cutting out the rearmost 4 feet of the chassis including the rear spring hangers. Even so the Mercedes was driven aboard by the author prior to its journey back to Leicester.

Above: Unlike a conventional goods vehicle which has its load placed over or between the axles, recovery vehicles have their load hung on the back at the end of an arm or hitch which acts like a lever. This can have the effect of overloading the rear axle and reducing the front axle load causing loss of steering. Faced with this problem, N.M.T. designed the Weight Shifter. Ballast weights fitted in the body of their Ford Transcontinental are moved hydraulically to re-distribute the weight proportionally between the axles. This lightens the load on the rear axles and increases the front axle loading or vice-versa whichever application is required.

Above right: Ward's Cargo was originally a box van in the United Biscuits delivery fleet before being converted for recovery work. Seen here with the burnt out remains of an 0813 Cargo curtainsider on board, it was fitted with a 6.5-ton slideback body, a 5-ton dp winch and a spectacle lift at the rear for a second vehicle lift and tow facility. A 3½- 5-ton Hiab was also fitted. Sadly the vehicle was stolen in 1993 from outside its owner's premises even though fitted with anti theft devices, proof that with the best will in the world, if someone wants it, they will steal it.

Right: Converted in 1986, Turners Ford Cargo is equipped with a Dyson Enforcer 10 underlift and is seen performing a rear end lift on a Leyland Atlantean bus used solely for recovery and training demonstrations. Turners hail from Sedgefield, Co. Durham.

Above: Albany's Cargo was powered by a Perkins V8 engine and was fitted with a Holmes 600 crane and a Ty-Rite underlift conversion. An interesting point is the position of the vertical exhaust, which emerges halfway down the body instead of behind the cab, as is the norm. Based near Birmingham's notorious 'Spaghetti Junction', this immaculate truck was a regular sight attending incidents on and around the busy intersection before being sold on to make way for another vehicle.

Above left: Marquiss of Scotland carved themselves a niche in the transporter market by producing low cost, good quality units like this one belonging to Motormove of Manchester. The basic requirements for a transporter are an angled deck with run up ramps and a winch for loading damaged or failed vehicles. The inclusion of a large crew cab for carrying the passengers of stranded vehicles make these vehicles ideal for relay work of the type carried out by the major motoring organisations.

Left: A Ford 9000 Series 6x4 operated as a recovery vehicle by Mick Gould Commercials. The smart Cat powered unit features Dominator 30 recovery equipment.

Above: A Ford Louisville 6x4 converted to a recovery vehicle featuring Bulldog recovery equipment by Wreckers International. Originally operated by Crouch Garage of Ashford, Kent on long distance fast recovery, it is currently working for the town's Willesborough & Kennington concern. The vehicle's lhd aspect is not seen as an impediment, more so a safety feature, especially with regard to Motorway work. Introduced in 1970, the 'L' family of conventional heavy trucks was available in a wide variety of 4x2 and 6x4 types with GM's V6 and Detroit Diesel's V8 being offered as options. This Cummins powered example was part of a consignment of chassis being shipped to Iran, but was landed in the U.K. when political events intervened in the shape of the Iranian revolution.

Gracing the Syren Recovery Equipment stand at the 1990 AVRO show was John Wall's 'Black Beauty', a 1981 Freightliner conventional which is equipped with a Holmes 750 crane and powered by a 350 Cummins engine. Joining a mixed fleet of over 20 recovery units, the vehicle is based in South Wales and is every inch an impressive working vehicle.

Above: During the 1970s, the Kenning Motor Group employed a fleet of Big J 6 recovery vehicles at various motorway services operated under the Kenning Group name. Powered by a Cummins 220 diesel, the tandem drive vehicles were fitted with a TFL T20 crane and an all-steel body. Each vehicle was also fitted with the distinctive TFL pattern front bumper which acts as a ballast weight as well as providing additional front-end protection to the cab. Many of the vehicles are still around today and one such example is shown here in the livery of Chatfields of Manchester, a Leyland Daf agent based in Ardwick.

Above right: After spending its revenue earning life hauling medical supplies for the Smith & Nephew group, this Big J 4T was purchased by a Toyota dealership and fitted with a Harvey Frost crane previously on a Ford D Series. Following a change in company policy, the Guy was sold to F. Dugdale & Sons of Nelson who in turn sold it to a local coach operator to replace an old Dodge wrecker similarly equipped. The photograph was taken shortly after Calder Coaches acquired the truck and shows it being prepared for a repaint.

Right: This Guy Big J 6 recovery vehicle belonging to J & A Smith of Maddiston, near Falkirk was photographed at their depot in June 1975. Now fitted with equipment by Harvey Frost, it is believed to be based on one of the two heavy haulage tractors the company employed for the delivery of new Caterpillar plant.

Right and above: Scotmech operate this pair of Ivecos, one from each of its Scottish depots. Aberdeen is supported by the 4-axle version, which is a stretched twin steer unit now fitted with a raisable fourth axle. The Dundee base is served by the 3-axle 190-48. Both trucks are fitted with the familiar Interstater underlift now marketed under the Boniface Engineering name, they taking over the mantle from Wreckers International in the manufacture and fitment of this very popular crane.

Top left: Geoff Rhodes, a commercial vehicle dealer from Market Harborough, bought this International Loadstar from a U.S. Government surplus sale. In service with British based U.S. Armed Forces, the immaculate truck had done little work prior to disposal but had been stripped of several components before release. Powered by the IH V8 diesel, the engine has an unusual trait when idling. A valve on the fuel pump shuts down 4 cylinders, producing a rather lumpy but distinctive tick-over. However, when the throttle is pressed the valve opens and all 8 cylinders come back on stream.

Above left: Another Loadstar from a surplus sale is this example belonging to Albany Motors. A Seventies model, the cab has been extensively re-modelled and a crew cab built from glass fibre. The hood and wings are a one-piece moulding and the eye-catching truck is fitted with a 5-ton underlift.

Left: Today's trend towards modern, stylish bodywork has led to a generation of look-alike vehicles. Most of the modern vehicles built today lack the individuality of their predecessors, the majority of which were individually styled, designed and built. Trimoco's Iveco carries the de-luxe body produced by Wreckers International and although sleek, it may be considered rather bland when compared with the AEC's of V.J.Harper and Granthams of Spalding.

Above: A novel concept developed by Boniface Engineering and fitted to Auto Recoveries 190-42 is the Sidewinder. This is a winch platform that can be swivelled into line with the casualty being recovered with the result of making side winching tasks less strenuous for the recovery vehicle. This is due to the fact that the winch rope is fed out direct from the winch drum to the casualty in a straight line and not down the length of the main jib, to the fairleads and then out, at an angle, to the vehicle in difficulty, thus creating a lever effect capable of slewing the recovery vehicle round. Side stabilisers are fitted with an additional set provided between the rear axles, the rearmost of which is non-driven and raisable.

Top left: John Macadam operates a fleet of recovery vehicles, some in connection with his accident repair business. One early member was EVW 65T, a 90m 57 Iveco powered by a 4-cylinder air-cooled diesel. The sets of wheels behind the cab are called dollies and are placed under the casualty enabling a full lift to be carried out. A full lift is when all the casualty's wheels are clear of the ground.

Above left: One of the smallest slideback systems available is the Hydraloader Minor 2 as fitted to this Iveco Daily. With a 2 tons capacity, the Minor 2 is designed to be fitted to a chassis of between 3 and 6 tons g.v.w. To keep load space to a maximum, the winch is fitted behind the rear axle underneath the deck with the winch cable running forward to a pulley mounted on the front bulkhead. The cable is then fed around this pulley and back down the deck to the casualty.

Left: Langer Park Service Station operated this Jeep J20 4x4 with a Bulldog Cruiser crane and lifting sling. The jib is extendable and can be locked in different heights by means of a pin in the slotted bar under the boom.

Above: 'Big Ivy' operated by Lancaster-based Pye Motors has a rather unusual axle configuration for an U.K. recovery vehicle. Although it is a 6x2, the second axle is a steered one rather than the more common fixed load bearing type. This configuration is popular in mainland Europe but has not yet gained acceptance here. The underlift is the TFL 'T' lift type and the truck is also fitted with a winch and spades.

Above: Dando's Kenworth is one of a small number of the marque imported into the U.K. in the early Eighties. The vehicle is right-hand drive and is again unusual by American specifications in only having a single rear axle. Dando's fitted the Brimec Centurion underlift, and the truck is pictured delivering a time expired LV-cabbed ERF recovery vehicle to the Roger Dyson Group headquarters at Redditch in Worcestershire.

Right: This Kenworth was imported into this country by Wreckers International for Richard Rolls of Sawfords Recovery. Equipment consists of a lattice boom Holmes 750 and a 10-ton underlift making this a very useful vehicle. Unusual in the U.K. is the twin gear-stick transmission fitted, giving the driver a multitude of gear ratios to chose from. The third axle is an air suspended tag type, popular on European trucks but rare on U.S. models; the double drive bogie still reigning supreme. The crane is now fitted with the square type booms and the vehicle is now with Newtyle Commercials.

Below right: 'Midnight Rider' started life as a V.I.T. (very important truck) Silver Edition tractor unit, built to commemorate 25 years of Kenworth in Canada. Equipped with a massive 108" double sleeper cab, the truck was converted to a recovery vehicle by Kenworth Trucks of Newbury, Berkshire. The crane is a Dominator 30 by Wreckers International and the truck has a striking custom livery depicting a smaller version breaking out of the side of the cab.

Below: Seen on the CJR stand at the 1995 AVRO exhibition was N.Y. Recoveries big and beautiful 6x4 Kenworth which was fitted with a Dominator twin boom crane, a three stage Liftmaster underlift and custom bodywork by S.V. Engineering. The Detroit powered truck had undergone a major refurbishment before being callously destroyed, along with several others, in an arson attack on its owner's premises.

Above: Converted from a time expired revenue earning vehicle, this Leyland Titan is typical of the type of recovery vehicle used for many years by municipal bus companies whose staff had the skill and expertise to carry out such conversions. Still retaining its half cab, the bodywork incorporates a workshop area to the rear and the open plan deck allows uninterrupted access to the Gar-Wood crane. The vehicle was retired in 1992/93 in favour of a brand new Seddon Atkinson Strato fitted with underlift equipment.

Above left: This ageing Leyland 12.8.1. Beaver recovery vehicle was still in use at ARC Quarries at Helston, Cornwall when photographed in June 1975. It dates originally from about 1948.

left: The once popular Land Rover has gone into a decline in the recovery world over the past few years. John Watson's example is one of a batch built from new by Wreckers International who fitted a Bulldog crane and an electric winch.

Right: Fearings Transport of Burnley were a long-established haulage company that was absorbed into the Green Line Group in the late Eighties. A one time flat in the Guinness distribution fleet, this 1960 Leyland Hippo was bought and converted in the company workshops to look after the 50 strong fleet which ran on general haulage. The fixed jib was fitted with a pulley to allow the winch rope to be run over the top to provide a lift for stranded vehicles. Originally powered by a Leyland 680 engine, a failure saw this ousted in favour of a 600 Power Plus which propelled the truck along at a sedate 30-mph. A serious accident befell the truck in 1983 and it was subsequently scrapped.

Left: Super Hippos were quite rare on British roads as most were built for export. This particular truck was part of a cancelled order and went to work for Siddle C. Cook of Consett, County Durham. Tom Carruthers later purchased the vehicle and converted it for recovery work by adding a Holmes W45 crane and a Diamond T body along with other ancillary equipment. Powered by a 680 diesel and with a choice of over 20 forward gear ratios, the truck has now been sold on by Tom who at the time of writing is President of the Road Rescue Recovery Organisation, (the three R's).

Below Left: Ribble Motor Services converted CRN 978 into a recovery vehicle in 1965. Having originally entered service in 1950, it was already 15 years old when given a new lease of life. The two manually deployed stiff legs on the Harvey Frost crane can be seen stored in the upright position next to the two lifting hooks. Receiving fleet number BD1 after conversion, the Leyland has now been preserved along with CRN 984, fleet number BD3.

Below: This rear view of the Martian featured opposite, shows the crane with the operators seat and controls mounted at the side. A two-speed Turner winch is fitted underneath the deck and the rope is pulled out by an auxiliary capstan winch. The crane, similar to the U.S. Austin Western type, will lift 15 tons with the stabilisers down. It slews through 240 degrees and underneath, at the back, is a spade anchor which is hydraulically raised and lowered and can withstand pulls of up to 30 tons.

Towards the end of the 1950s, a heavy recovery tractor
was developed for the British Army based on a chassis
already in service as a gun tractor. Powered by the Rolls
Royce B81 8-cylinder petrol engine and designated
FV1119, it had a rear drive axle layout similar to the
Scammell Explorer. With a top speed of 30 mph, a petrol
consumption of 3 miles to the gallon and a ready-to-go
weight of around 22 tons, the Leyland Martian was

Left: NTC 172G was owned by British Nuclear Fuels Ltd until it was bought by Gilbraith Commercials in the early Eighties to replace an elderly, worn out Leyland Hippo. Fitted with a crude 3-ton jib, the truck only saw limited use until it was sold to Burrows Haulage of Simonstone near Burnley. With recovery becoming more specialised, it was decided that the equipment was inadequate and the high investment required to replace it was unjustified. The Accrington depot decided to use the services of a specialist company for recovery so they could concentrate on their core business of selling and repairing Leyland Daf trucks.

Below left: Another member of Boardman's diverse fleet is this workman-like Leyland Buffalo. Photographed when it was based at Forton Services on the M6, the crane is believed to be the only one of its type in service. The two chains visible at the rear of the crane jib are connected to internal rams, which are independently controlled and are used to lift the rear 'A' frame. The large gear sprocket is attached to the winch which is chain driven from a separate hydraulic motor. Seeing the exposed drive mechanism, one wonders what has happened to the safety guard.

Left: Millers of Longton near Preston, Lancs are long established recovery operators who are now involved in the design and construction of recovery units for other operators. Seen here is an example which they built and operated in their own recovery fleet based on a Cummins-powered Leyland Marathon chassis. The crane is a 10-ton rated underlift fitted with hydraulic spades and a Gar-Wood winch is also fitted. As well as carrying out recovery duties for Millers, the truck doubled as a demonstrator for those operators who are interested in purchasing one of John's cranes.

Above: When the time came to replace their ageing Matador, the Burnley & Pendle Bus Company purchased KAO 556D, a 1966 Leyland Hippo, and set about designing and building their own underlift. Upon completion of the crane and after its subsequent fitting to the chassis, it was passed over to the company's bodyshop for the bodywork, the design of which incorporates roller shutter doors on the tool lockers. All the work was done 'in house' and is testament to the variety of skills possessed by many bus company personnel whose diversity of talents keep their fleets operational.

Above: Photographed in the Alfreton, Derbyshire yard of the crane hire company, Grayston, White & Sparrow, this vehicle is not all it seems. Whilst the front-end is a Leyland Marathon, the rear end is a Diamond T. Both halves were grafted together by a company in Brigend, Glamorgan who were subsequently taken over by G.W & S. The vehicle was transferred to Alfreton and then to their Derby depot. Renowned for its power when towing mobile cranes, it was also reputed to have a top speed in excess of 70 mph when travelling solo. The truck has now been disposed off.

Above: Evans's Marathon is fitted with an EKA underlift and a curvilinear body. Due to the body being previously fitted on a shorter vehicle, a distance piece has been added to fill the gap between the back of the cab and the front of the body. Chequer plate has been added to the bottom of the lockers in order to protect the bodywork when removing or stowing items of equipment.

Above right: The thrills and spills of motor racing have always proved exciting, but when it goes wrong the task of clearing up falls to the track marshals and stewards. At the Silverstone Racing Circuit this task was aided by their Leyland Terrier fitted with a Harvey Frost crane. Although only used at the circuit, the officials placed great faith in the little Terrier and are proud of the fact that some of the greatest names have ended up being rescued by this truck. No matter how famous you are, a breakdown or accident can be a great leveller.

Right: The most common range of commercial vehicles operating in this country falls into the 7.5-17 ton range. To cater for their recovery, equipment manufacturers have produced a 5-ton underlift that is adequate for this task. This alleviates the need for operators to purchase the more expensive larger capacity units. Queens Motors Roadrunner has a Guardian 5 ton with spec frame attachments fitted onto the crosshead thus allowing cars and vans to be recovered also.

AB Trucks at Reading have this short wheelbase Landtrain fitted with Interstater recovery equipment on hand to handle their emergencies. This is an example of several recovery units built on Landtrain chassis by Wreckers International, some of which, prior to their conversion, had previously worked on the Mount Pleasant construction project in the Falklands. The location is Donington Park racing circuit.

Right: This Leyland 16-13 supplied to one of the London bus operators features EKA's D Series heavy highway recovery unit designed for bus recovery, it has a hydraulic boom extension of 0.6m enabling it to reach set back axles. Retracted boom lift capacity is 9 tonnes. The vehicle also carries a 7 tonne winch.

Below right: Arcade are a large recovery company based in London and are specialists in the re-patriation of damaged vehicles from all over Europe. Much of the work nearer home involves negotiating the badly congested streets of our capital city. TKE 261X was once engaged on this task. Its short length made it more manoeuvrable round the streets but this also reduced its lifting capacity to about 5 or 6 tons. Even so, this was still adequate for the vast majority of delivery vehicles found in a city environment.

Below: Egertons' Leyland is a bit of a wolf in sheep's clothing. The crane is a Bulldog Recoverer and is one of the first of its type. Originally fitted to a Scammell Crusader for Glasgow-based Thomas Ash by Wreckers International, the cab was destroyed by fire. So what Egertons undertook in their Mobberley workshop was to remove the Crusader front-end and graft the Leyland one in its place, so in effect creating a hybrid. The steps in the bodywork are to allow the operator to gain access to the control console just visible at the rear of the crane.

Another of Les Wallings creations, this time a Leyland Daf 95 which was bought with an accident damaged cab. Wallings fitted a new cab, extended the chassis and fitted a Volvo double drive bogie before installing the Holmes 750 twin boom crane, the new Interstater underlift and the lockered body. The photograph was taken after Wallings had delivered their Renault Magnum, which can just be seen inside the workshop, to JDS Trucks for an engine repair.

Above: Walling's Daf 95 started out as a twin steer tractor unit before being stretched and fitted with a Volvo F10 double drive bogie. The Dominator twin boom crane was previously fitted to an AEC Mandator but required the booms lengthening in order to make everything look proportional when installed. This was duly done and an Interstater underlift was added with a double extension for recovering coaches which is a Les Walling speciality.

Above right: Dragons 380 bhp Daf 95 is fitted with a crane built by the Italian company, Omars. It has an overlift capacity of 40 ton and a 3-stage underlift. The most interesting feature of the crane is the fact that the entire drop arm and folding arm are part of the inner extension which means when the jib is extended, the whole underlift section goes with it.

Right: John Canham's Daf is seen leaving the yard of JDS Trucks with one of East Coast Carriers in tow. John's Daf is equipped with a Century 5030T and was built by World Wide Recovery Systems, a member of the Lantern Group in Hertford. Century cranes are very popular in the U.S.A and it is only recently that they have become widely available over here. Century are part of Miller Industries who also own other manufacturers, including Challenger, Holmes and more recently Boniface to name but a few.

Left: Billington's Daf 95 is fitted with a Brimec self levelling underlift and commercial wheel grids. Because of the extreme length of the body and the possibility of its flexing when under load, the designers at Roger Dysons have built the body sides in two separate sections. The first section comprises the main lockers and the second, over the rear wheels, comprises the supplementary and control lockers. The separation can be seen just in front of the third axle.

Below left: Photographed at Seddon-Atkinson Commercials of Airdrie, Scotland in March 1976, all is not what it first appears. This six-wheel wrecker is in fact a Mack featuring a cleverly mounted Atkinson Mk 2 fibreglass cab and Atkinson cast radiator.

Below: John Boardman's 'Super Mack' was fitted with a hydraulic extending boom crane and a front mounted Gar-Wood winch. To provide stability when lifting, a pair of semi-trailer landing legs were fitted at the rear, these could be wound down when required but had to be raised for lift and tow duties. Powered by a Rolls diesel, the Mack was last seen languishing in Millers of Longton's yard, devoid of lifting gear and engine, awaiting a decision on its future.

Above: A bonneted Mack recovery vehicle from the fleet of Walls Truck Services featuring Holmes gear. With bases in the Newport and Aust services, Walls' trucks provide emergency cover for amongst other places, the Severn Bridge where high winds frequently play havoc with crossing traffic. The R type served with P & D Cosby for a short while before entering Walls fleet. The company also ran a FM cabover model fitted with Bulldog recovery gear.

Right: Billington Brothers Mack was once owned by J.B. Rawcliffe, the heavy haulage specialist, where it had been used as a 150-ton prime mover. Roger Dyson fitted the Enforcer 15 crane and the well-proportioned bodywork before the truck was brought north to begin its second life. This rear view shows the maximum height of the two-stage boom with the underlift folded down and extended. The rear spades can also be seen in the lowered position.

Left and below: Once the pride of the Mike Lawrence heavy haulage fleet based in Highbridge, Somerset and now the flagship of the Albany Motors fleet based in Gateshead, UYC 39W is fitted with a Syren 3-stage underlift and hydraulic outriggers. Behind the extended front bumper sits a heavy duty Morris winch, but to the rear is a custom designed and built slewing winch which is ideal for jobs where a side pull is required. For really heavy-duty winching, a Darlington winch is mounted at the front of the body.

Above: This DM Series Mack operated by D+G Cars is believed to have started its working life on a construction site in Dubai before finding its way to the U.K. Now equipped with a Bro underlift and a Hojberg crane, the most striking feature of the truck is the cab which is offset to the left. This is a curious trait of some of the Mack 'conventionals' which are blessed with a notoriously narrow cab, access to which is via the steps formed in the fuel tanks.

Above: VRA 284S has led a very chequered but well documented life. As a heavy haulage unit it has served in the fleets of West of Scotland Excavations, A.F. Budge and W.J. & D. Demolition. Now, minus its sleeper box, it has entered the fleet of Wakefield Autos based in Boston, Lincs. Overhauled in the company workshops, the 6x4 unit is now fitted with a custom-made body and underlift designed and built in-house by the staff at Wakefields whose skill and eye for detail helped create an eye catching truck.

Above right: Situated on the A59 near Ripon, North Yorkshire, is Monkton Moor Garage, home of this splendid 6x4 Magirus Deutz. The custom made hydraulic jib is complimented by two Boughton winches alongside which are the upright exhaust pipes from the air-cooled V10 diesel.

Right: Graham Ward has had good service from his fleet of M.A.Ns. This 16-170 came from the Cow & Gate fleet and was originally fitted with a fridge body. Dysons fitted the Hydraloader slideback and the 6.5 ton/metre Hiab crane. Seen on board is an elderly petrol-engined J type Bedford with a hydraulic jib and lifting sling. This was in service with Weldbank Garage of Chorley and was on its way for disposal when photographed.

Left and left below: Perrins Commercials of Walsall used this ingenious crane which they had fitted to an M.A.N. 16-280 tractor unit. Called the Hudlift 2200, it fits onto the existing 5th wheel and is raised by an integral power pack connected to the 7 pin electrical suisie. This provides power lift, gravity lower and a manual extension. Holmes offer a similar model and both can be fitted in a few minutes, thus converting a standard tractor unit into a lift and tow recovery vehicle. The crane appeals to many fleet operators because they do not need to purchase an expensive recovery vehicle, which may only see occasional use.

Right: Once a Dunkerley Transport 6x4 heavy haulage unit, John Walls' impressive M.A.N rescue unit 'Master of Disaster' - now boasts a self-steer air suspended second axle, a 20 ton underlift, twin winches, a slewing crane and the large front bumper incorporates a 15 ton winch. Design and build was by Steve Young's team at Syren Engineering. The whole system can be operated remotely allowing the operator a greater degree of flexibility and safety.

Below: George Mutch operates several lightweight M.A.N's in his Perth-based fleet, amongst which is this 8.136 equipped with a Century crane and wheel lift, together with twin winches. It was built by Wreckers International.

Above: After towing this damaged Volvo artic outfit weighing in at 38 tons from Stoke-on-Trent to Lancashire, Wards M.A.N 17-291 pauses whilst awaiting parking instructions at its final destination. The vehicle started life as a 4x2-drawbar unit for Silcocks Express, the vehicle delivery company, the chassis was lengthened and a double drive bogie fitted before being dispatched to Roger Dyson for the fitment of the Enforcer crane and bodywork. Twin Boughton winches are fitted along with a remote control unit allowing freedom of movement for the operator.

Right: Commercial Vehicle Services 16-331 is a 6x2 with a pusher axle. The 8.5-ton underlift was built by the Lifting Gear Specialist Group of Leigh in Lancs. CVS are a M.A.N main dealer based in Manchester.

Right below: Not all twin boom equipped trucks are big machines. Gerard Mann's 813 fitted with Bulldog 10 equipment proves that. This well proportioned little truck is more than capable of handling small trucks and vans which constitute a large proportion of the goods vehicles on the road today.

Below: Ian Gordon's Irish registered 19-362 is powered by the D2866 engine coupled to a ZF Ecosplit 16-speed gearbox. The 13.5 ton rear axle is air suspended and the crane was built by Willinghams of Thorngumbald. Two Ramsey winches are fitted, a 10 ton which is routed through the boom centre and a 12 ton auxiliary one which is directed over the offside stiff leg. The vehicle is based at Dalrymple in Ayrshire.

Left: Christened 'Micks Mighty Merc', this Mercedes 1624 4x4 truck was driven by the author throughout its life in the UK. Imported in 1989 from Denmark where it had operated in the red livery of the Falks Redningskorps, the state run emergency organisation, the truck was equipped with an 8 ton underlift and a 35 ton, 4 speed winch. In 1991, the chassis was retired but the crane lives on and is now fitted to the Renault of JDS Trucks at Blackburn.

Right: It seems only right and proper that a Mercedes main dealer should operate a marque recovery vehicle. Ciceley's 1977 model 1629 has a Wreckmaster twin boom with a similar capacity to the Holmes 600.

Left below: Autotow of Hyde, Cheshire have a very striking livery and their vehicles are always kept very clean. Shown here is a new 609D fitted with crew cab and a Hydralift 2000 spec lift enabling cars and vans up to 2-ton axle weight to be recovered.

Below: Egerton's diverse fleet includes this extended 1626 tractor unit which is fitted with Interstater recovery gear and wheel scotches instead of hydraulic spades. Full use has been made of the body for locker storage The vehicle is based at Sandbach Services on the M6 motorway.

99

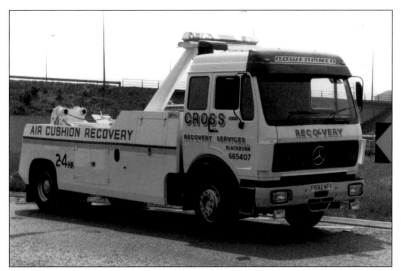

Above: Another member of the Macadam's fleet is F130 XEA, an 814 fitted with a Whitacres crew cab and a Dyson Hydraloader slideback. Fitted with an extra fuel tank, this vehicle is used mainly on relay work for the motoring clubs and is a regular visitor to the south of England, ferrying stranded vehicles and passengers to their home destinations.

Above left: At one time, Blackburn-based Cross Recovery Services operated two of these 1644 Powerliners equipped with E.P.S. gearboxes. Both were fitted with Mk 2 Interstater underlifts, twin winches and both were built as recovery vehicles from new. The sister vehicle was sold making way for a new arrival and entered service with the Lantern Group. Sadly, F692 WFV had a more ignominious end; it was stolen from its owner's yard in March 1991 and never retrieved.

Left: Lurking in the Lincolnshire countryside is this giant Oshkosh owned by Billingborough Tractors and Commercials. Powered by a six cyl. turbocharged Cat diesel engine coupled to a Fuller Roadranger gearbox, it has an auxiliary gearbox giving over 30 forward gear ratios. The recovery equipment was built in-house consisting of a hydraulic underlift backed up by a Tulsa winch. To keep the front axle on the ground, nearly three tons of ballast weights have been added, these can be seen alongside and underneath the hefty front bumper.

Above: Square One's Oshkosh served the York branch of BRS for many years before being bought by Highway Recovery. Built in South Africa, the truck was eventually imported into the UK and spent some time working in a quarry in Glamorgan before travelling north to Yorkshire. The crane has a lift capacity of approximately 7 tons and is capable of slewing if required. After purchasing the truck from Highway, Square One Commercials of Barnstaple, North Devon totally re-furbished the vehicle, in the process giving it a custom paint job that no photograph can do justice to.

Left: Compare this picture with Sawfords Diamond T seen earlier, both vehicles are 6x4 bonneted American trucks fitted with twin boom equipment, but there the similarity ends for here is a beautifully turned out Peterbilt with a Holmes 750. The registration number Q999 WRX also graced 'Classy Lady', another of Sawfords Peterbilts.

Right: Shown here is the 'Classy Lady', a 6x4 Peterbilt in the livery of Sawfords of Maidenhead. It is fitted with a three-stage 40-ton American Challenger crane and a Guardian underlift. Painted in a metallic blue and white colour scheme, the truck was kept in immaculate condition by Richard Rolls, the company proprietor. The vehicle is now owned by R.U.D. Recovery of Cradley Heath.

Below: Still in the colours of CGL Truck Services, a now defunct Renault main dealer, is this TR305 fitted with a TFL underlift and basic steel body. The familiar TFL counter weight adorns the front bumper. Later owned by JDS Trucks and operated from their Salford depot, the vehicle was captured on film recovering a Mercedes van with a failed gearbox.

Above: By contrast with CGL's Renault, Arcades R340 has the uprated version of the same cab. The main differences being the absence of rear windows, the addition of marker lights above the windscreen, a revised interior and a more powerful engine. Fitted with a Mk 3 Interstater incorporating an integral coach beam and twin winches, this particular truck featured in Wreckers International's sales literature for the Mk 3 crane and was reputed to have a static lift capacity, with the spades deployed and the arm retracted, of 25 tons.

Above left: Eager to enter the light recovery vehicle market, Renault UK commissioned Roger Dyson to build a Hydralift 1500 on a new B110 demonstrator. This is an uprated version of the familiar Master range but has rear-wheel drive and is fitted with dual rear tyres, giving the vehicle a g.v.w. of 4 tons, which allows vehicles with an axle weight of up to 1.5 tons to be recovered without overloading its own rear axle.

Left: This 1983 model R310 was previously a tractor unit engaged on continental tanker haulage before being converted for recovery work in 1991. The crane and winch were taken from the 4x4 Mercedes of Graham Ward previously shown and the bodywork was constructed with the assistance of Technical Engineering Services based at Great Harwood. Now owned by JDS Trucks at Blackburn, the cab underwent a major refurbishment in 1994 when it was fitted with the later type one piece front grille.

Above: The Renault Magnum is an impressive truck by any standards. Not happy with that, Kenfield commissioned Boniface Recovery Systems to build them what is believed to be the first 8 wheeled Magnum in the world. Originally a 4x2 tractor powered by the 420 ace engine coupled to a TBV semi-automatic gearbox, the truck was stretched and fitted with two extra safe air suspended axles. The second axle is a self-steer and locks in the straight-ahead position when reverse gear is engaged and the third axle is coupled to the trucks own computerised Airtronic suspension system. The recovery equipment is complimented by 'cab command' which allows some of the cranes operations to be carried out from inside the cab with the aid of a close circuit television system.

Left: Arcade's 420 6x2 is thought to be the first Magnum in the UK to be converted. Fitted with a Boniface Recoverer, the designer has taken care to ensure the bodywork is kept in proportion with the large, tall cab, something achieved to great effect. The unit is designed for long distance towing and is expected to spend much of its time travelling to and from Europe.

Below left: S & H purchased this lhd Magnum as a 4x2 tractor unit. They promptly set about stretching the chassis and adding two SAF air suspended lift axles before sending the vehicle to Boniface Engineering for equipment to be fitted. This came in the guise of a Recoverer Maxireach underlift with a 30 ton capacity extending top boom, two 30,000 lb H30 Superwinches and deluxe bodywork. The Maxireach is so called because it extends to 4.4. metres.

Below: Developed in 1927 but not ordered by the military until 1936, the Pioneer was built primarily as an articulated tank transporter or as gun tractor. It was this variant that was adapted to become a heavy recovery unit and was originally equipped with a collapsible jib. The vast majority were eventually fitted with the sliding jib that was later used on the Explorer.

The Pioneer's successor - the Explorer. Basically a development of the Pioneer utilising its predecessors suspension but with the advantage of 6x6 drive. This fine example found further work with the Wiltshire garage after military release at the beginning of the Seventies.

Above: Critchley's Scammell Crusader is fitted with a much-modified cab and has been disguised to look like an American cabover. The Rolls powered truck is fitted with an underlift built by an engineering company in Wales. It also has a chain driven Gar-Wood winch, and a hydraulic Boughton 250 winch.

Although externally the cab may look modern, underneath it is showing its age and has succumbed to corrosion, and is due to be replaced with a newer cab in the near future, although whether or not it will be customised like this one, remains to be seen.

Above: Frodsham Motors own this well kept Constructor which was built about 1960 and is fitted with a Harvey Frost Atlas 12 crane and a 15-ton vertical spindle winch. The Atlas 12 was the only hydraulic crane offered by Harvey Frost and as the name implies, it had a 12-ton lifting capacity. The saw-tooth arrangement on the two uprights are to hold an adjustable cross bar on which the jib rests when carrying out suspended tows.

Above right: The Scammell Trunker was a 6x2 twin-steer tractor unit which could be fitted with a choice of engines. The second axle was fitted with air bellows that allowed weight to be transferred onto the drive axle if traction became a problem. This version was owned by Hygrade Recovery of Oldham and was formerly in service with Wilsons Brewery. The lifting equipment comprises a hydraulic jib on top of which is a pull out extension which can be pinned at various lengths depending on requirements.

Right: The Explorer was the standard British Armed Forces recovery tractor of the 50s and 60s. Powered by a 10-litre Meadows petrol engine, the Scammell was blessed with excellent cross-country capability. Recovery equipment consisted of a 15 ton vertical spindle winch mounted underneath the body and a 3-ton hand actuated sliding jib. After being 'de mobbed' the Explorer found favour with civilian operators, many of whom fitted a Gardner diesel engine in a bid to improve on the 2-3 mpg achieved by the thirsty 6 cylinder petrol engine.

Left: Egerton's Scammell Crusader is based at their Cumbria depot near Workington and features a single extending boom crane manufactured by Century. Built for British Airways, it was used to recover various vehicles operated in the air freight division and ground support fleet. It was eventually replaced by an Interstater equipped Scania.

Below left: In the early Seventies, the British Army carried out extensive trials with EKA recovery gear fitted to a Volvo chassis. So successful was this trial that it was decided to purchase the crane and body for fitment to the Crusader chassis. In 1976, an order for 130 of these units was placed and by the mid Eighties, the order was completed and the trucks deployed. As the Crusader was only a 6x4, and lacked front wheel drive capabilities, it was classed as a low mobility recovery vehicle. As ever with 'de-mobbed' military recovery vehicles, they become much sought after by civilian operators. Berkley's Scammell is one such example.

Below: John Millers V8 Detroit powered Crusader has had the chassis extensively stretched and a heavy-duty underlift built in the company workshops at Longton. A Gar-Wood winch is fitted which is driven through a Ford 4-speed gearbox. For side winching, a sliding shoe is fitted to the top of the main boom for the cable to return to. Side stabilisers are concealed behind doors fitted in the fully lockered bodywork.

Scammell trucks always sold well overseas where they had a reputation for being reliable under severe operating conditions. Power came from either Rolls Royce, Cummins or as in A.S. Whitaker's truck, a V8 Detroit Diesel. Also offered were a 40-ton rear bogie and a 15-speed Fuller gearbox. TTG 762Y was registered in 1983 and built in left-hand-drive configuration. The warning 'do not paint' on the front grille is to allow smooth operation of the radiator blind which opens and closes automatically to aid engine warm-up from cold.

Above: A long term Scammell devotee is David Crouch of Lutterworth in Leicestershire. Seen here is one of the later breed of trucks in his fleet. It is a left-hand-drive S26 which has been extended and fitted with twin boom crane and Interstater underlift.

Above left: George Mutch's S26 is a heavy-duty version of the Leyland Roadtrain and shares certain components with its lightweight stablemate. Powered by a 350 Cummins engine coupled to a Spicer transmission, the truck has a train weight of 80 tons. The underlift is the ubiquitous Interstater model and winching is undertaken by the two 15 ton Rotzlers fitted. The photograph was taken in 1986, just prior to the vehicle entering service.

Left: Faced with the problem of a severely corroded cab shell on his Scammell Contractor, Alan Sime of Newtyle Commercials, Dundee searched for an alternative and settled upon a redundant Bedford TM cab to resolve his problem. The resulting conversion you can see here. The vehicle is fitted with recovery gear from a AEC Militant, and carries the name of 'Bonzo the Bear', (not to be confused with Chris Miller's Mack of the same name).

Above: Somerset Rescue's massive Scammell S24 has something of a chequered history. Now based on the A38 at Biddisham but previously with the Essex Fire & Rescue Service, it was known to everyone as 'Big Red'. However, the resentment felt by many in the recovery industry, who objected to the fire brigade diversifying into what is a highly skilled branch of the motor trade, plus the fact that taxpayer's money had funded this behemoth, made its short service life with the brigade a very politically charged one. Fitted with Concept 3000 recovery gear and a Hap 910 loading crane, the truck was originally intended to be a tank transporter tractor but was never adopted so it was sold when the Scammell Works at Watford closed. It is powered by a 14-litre Cummins engine driving through an Allison automatic gearbox. Fuel consumption of the 6x6 unit is reckoned to be about 3 miles to the gallon.

Above: Danny Cross commissioned Wreckers International to build him the ultimate recovery vehicle on this ex military demonstrator Scammell S26 6x6 which is Rolls-powered and has a ZF automatic gearbox. Wreckers built and fitted a Concept 3000 3 stage overlift boom, an Interstater underlift, a 12 ton Atlas loading crane, four 15 ton winches and proceeded to transform the truck into the leviathan illustrated here. A fire damaged the cab early in its life and after refurbishment the vehicle was sold to the Lantern Group who were still operating it at the time of writing.

Right: Greater Manchester buses operate several recovery vehicles within their vast engineering department. Shown here is their 8x4 Constructor 30-26 which is fitted with an Interstater underlift and a 10 ton winch. Although liveried in G.M. Buses colours, the trucks are available for the recovery of other operator's vehicles and can be seen regularly towing trucks and buses throughout the North West. The Allison auto gearbox fitted makes life that little easier for the driver.

Below right: The Lantern group of Potters Bar now manufacture recovery units for other companies. In their own fleet is this Cummins 400-powered Scammell 33-40 fitted with a Holmes 750 and Interstater underlift. The length of the vehicle requires the booms to be used with the inner extensions pulled out to the first position. This allows the winch ropes to fall clear of the rear body panels. Built as an export model in left-hand drive configuration, the truck is also fitted with heavy-duty front wheels.

Below: This S24 appeared at the 1985 AVRO show in the drab desert livery of the British Army. Now excused military duties, it is in the livery of its new owners when photographed. The telescopic recovery crane and associate equipment was to be offered as an addition to the S24 range in the Scammell catalogue. The 1989 closure put paid to that.

Above: Built for J.B. Rawcliffe, the heavy haulage operator, and then bought by Billington Brothers of Manchester, 'Big Sue' is a 6x4 Scania 140 fitted with a Holmes 750. Once driven by Ernie Hesketh, the cab is covered in a multitude of lights and the light bar carries the legend 'Ernie loves Sue'.

Above left: In contrast to the sharp squared lines of S & H's Scania (page 118), George's older 110 has more rounded features and looks less aggressive, despite the formidable front bumper which also houses a winch. An interesting feature of the Scandinavian curvilinear bodywork is that it is considerably narrower than the overall vehicle width as determined by the wheels. This has the effect of keeping the body sides away from protruding objects that would otherwise have a tendency to damage the paint and panels. The car spec grid and rigid tow bar can be seen stowed on special brackets underneath the body.

Left: A one time member of David Crouch's fleet, Q423 ENR was bought by Dod Howland of Auto Recoveries (UK), who incidentally also bought Crouch's AEC Militant. The truck is a left-hand drive 141 model and has the lattice boom Holmes 750. Dod panelled the booms and also designed and constructed the underlift that is now fitted. Worthy of note is a legend on the door which proudly boasts 34 years experience and over 26,000 recoveries. This is indeed a record to be proud of.

One of the first Enforcer 15 cranes built by Roger Dyson was fitted to this ex heavy haulage Scania 141. Because of the large amount of space required for the equipment lockers, the twin fuel tanks have been re-sited behind the cab with access being gained via the steps over the air tanks and battery boxes. Egertons had this vehicle based on Sandbach Services for many years and it was frequently called upon to render assistance at accidents on this Cheshire stretch of the M6.

Above: The crane on this short wheelbase 112-cabbed Scania is somewhat dwarfed by the large cab. However, the compact design makes it ideal for the narrow lanes which are to be found in South Devon where the truck is based.

Above right: Recovery vehicle bodywork comes in many guises, from the sophisticated curvilinear, fully lockered bodies to the simple but functional budget body as demonstrated by Erikson's Scania. The Interstater crane and winch are more readily visible and there is a minimum amount of locker space, this suggests that only the minimal amount of equipment is carried.

Right: Frodsham Motors rare Scania 145 is believed to have started life a demonstrator for Wreckers International extolling the virtues of the Bulldog Dominator hydraulic twin boom crane. The vehicle is now owned by Cannon Commercials.

Left: S & H Recovery bought their 400 bhp 142 from a dealer in Holland as a tractor unit. After importation the vehicle was stretched and sent to Wreckers International for the crane and body to be fitted. Based at their Ferrybridge site on the A1, the truck was photographed attending a Mercedes 814 belonging to Fagan & Whalley which had suffered a radiator failure. S & H operate a large fleet of recovery vehicles, dealing with anything from a car to a maximum weight artic.

Left: Used as a heavy haulage tractor unit in the Bruce Cook road planning fleet until being extensively damaged in an accident, Sewell's Scania was bought and repaired at their Bishop Auckland base before being sent to Syren Engineering who built the triple extending underlift and fabricated the bodywork. There are facilities for working the crane and winches from a console at the front of the body, access to which is gained via the steps behind the nearside exhaust stack.

Below left: Seen at the Woolley Edge Services on the M1 Motorway was this 85-ton g.t.w. Scania 143 fitted with Wreckers International Concept 3000 recovery equipment. Operated by Highway Recovery, the truck is one of a large fleet operating from sites on the M1, M62 and A1 motorways. All of Highway's trucks are painted bright red with yellow cranes and are extremely well cared for.

Below: Worldwide's 4 Series Scania demonstrator shows off its Century underlift and the clean lines of their Super deluxe bodywork. The Scania cab is one of the most aesthetically pleasing currently in production and Worldwide have used it to their advantage in the design of this unit.

Built in June 1997 for the Mansfield Group by Boniface Engineering, this 4 Series Scania is fitted with a Mk 3E Interstater underlift and a 1060 Century Rotator (what we would call a slewing crane). Two 35,000lb dp winches are also fitted. Worthy of note is the way the designer has secured the body panel to the outrigger which is deployed when the crane is working over the side.

Left: The new 4 Series Scania is an impressive truck and no more so than Castle Recoveries 144-530 4-axle version. Kitted out again by Boniface, the south coast-based vehicle has been built with European recovery in mind.

Below left: Built by Barry Greenall, 'Conan the Shifter' was a 1976 Cummins-powered Seddon Atkinson 400. The crane jib was constructed using the main arm off a Hymac loading shovel. An internal jib extension has been fitted and this required a slight modification to the rear of the boom in order to accommodate it. This truck served Barry for many years before being replaced by a home-built under-lift, again on a Seddon Atkinson.

Below: Spurred on by his previous successes at building trucks for himself, Barry proceeded to construct 'The Legend'. Built as a joint project between himself and Millers of Longton, the 320 Cummins-powered truck started life as a 6x2 twin-steer tractor unit. The second steer axle was removed and a much modified air-lift tag axle from a Volvo was installed in its place. The bodywork was designed by its owner who utilised every bit of space available for equipment storage. Night time shows this truck to be a myriad of orange marker lights. The vehicle is now owned by Standish Service Station of Wigan.

Above: Photographed returning to its Stoke-on-Trent base after yet another successful recovery mission, is Jon Beech's Seddon Atkinson which is fitted with a heavy underlift and bodywork built by ACB Hydraulics. The recovered Volvo ran into the back of another heavy goods vehicle causing severe damage to both vehicles. Fortunately the driver suffered only minor injuries and was able to contact his boss to inform him of his predicament whilst rescuers released him from the cab. This is the damaged artic previously seen being towed by Wards M.A.N.

Above: Bought to operate in the harsh environment of the Peak District, Lamb & Mansfield's 8x8 Terberg, which sports a Volvo F7 cab, is a most impressive recovery unit. Equipped by Norfolk-based Boniface Engineering, it is fitted with an Interstater underlift, twin 25 ton Rotzler heavy duty winches and a Bonifiglioli crane which can reach up to 40 feet. Although built primarily as an on or off-road heavy recovery unit, damage free towing can be carried out if required.

Above: Steyr trucks had a very short reign in the UK market, having never achieved the popularity the manufacturer expected. Relatively few top weight tractor units were sold and a top weight recovery vehicle on one of these chassis is quite a rare find. John Wall's 19 S 31 is fitted with the high top cab and was fitted with the Enforcer 15 crane and bodywork by Roger Dyson.

Above right: Built in 1970, Wards N86 was operated by the Swedish 'Karen' recovery organisation. Fitted with a Holmes 750 twin boom crane, it was quite rare amongst Swedish recovery operators who have a tendency to favour the underlift unit for both lift and tow as well as major accident recovery. Powered by the TD70 engine, it was equipped with heating elements fitted in the sump, radiator and water jackets. This enabled the truck to be plugged into a domestic electrical socket to keep the engine at working temperature when parked overnight in the extreme cold of the Scandinavian winters, thus avoiding the need to defrost the vehicle every morning.

Right: Compare the squared off lines and sharp corners of Roger Giles & Sons N1027, with the rounded features of Wards N86, and you can see a sharp contrast in the way vehicle design changed in the 70s. The N86 was a development of the old Titan range whereas the N range was a new design featuring a taller cab and squarer bonnet. One of Roger Giles specialities is underwater recovery; this being carried out by a number of staff who are also trained divers.

Left: Fitted with a 5 ton Guardian underlift, Douthwaite's F86 was bought to replace their ageing AEC Mammoth Major. The bottom arm on this crane is lowered by a steel cable connected to a hydraulic ram mounted on top of the main boom, the other end being secured to the arm itself. When the ram is extended, the cable lengthens and the arm is lowered gently to the floor. To stow the arm, the ram is shortened and the cable tightened, thus raising the arm to its stored position.

Below left: Although sporting a genuine Holmes nameplate, another Holmes, Alan Holmes built the equipment on this Volvo, for use in his truck repair business. It consists of a single hydraulic jib with an extension and a chequer plate body. Other extras included are a modified headlamp arrangement, an alloy bumper and upright exhaust stacks.

Below: Owned from new by British Nuclear Fuels, this early 240 bhp F88 is equipped with a Wreckmaster 30 crane which has a similar capacity to the Holmes 750. Now owned by Tebay Vehicle Repairs of Cumbria, it was photographed with the remains of a Volvo F7 tractor unit which had just been recovered from a motorway embankment.

Above: Located at the Motherwell depot of W & J Riding and liveried in that haulier's colours, Mcintyre & Elder's F88 was privately owned by the company that maintained Riding's Scotland-based fleet. It was built originally for Parks of Hamilton, the Scottish coach operator, by Richards & Marsh of Wednesbury in the West Midlands. The 6x2 truck has an extending jib, a Gar-Wood winch and a gross train weight of 48 tons.

Above: Walling's Volvo started life as a tractor unit undertaking runs to the Middle East in 1981. One of a pair built at the Broughton workshops, the crane and body were all constructed 'in house'. Wallings specialise in continental coach recovery and this truck made several trips across the water before being sold to make way for the Foden illustrated previously. Cambell Commercials of Alexandria purchased the vehicle for use in their used truck business.

Above left: Durham City Recovery is the grand title displayed on Ian Bradley's F12. The underlift and body were built by a company who also have a grand title, Willinghams of Thorngumbald, which is near Hull. Although the body style implies a curvilinear type, it is merely an outer skin, with lockers being inserted at strategic points as requested by the customer. No rear spades are fitted, instead there are stiff legs that have flat feet, and these cause less damage when lowered to the ground during heavy lift operations.

Left: M & D Transport's F88 has hydraulic gear loosely built along the lines of the TFL T20. A departure from the norm is the sloping lockers which housed the associated equipment required. It was photographed at the company's depot taking on fuel for its next run.

Above: Q59 VOE now operates in the fleet of South Scotland Coachworks. It was purchased from Albany Recovery Services who, for many years, used it as their main accident response vehicle. The combination of the Holmes 750 and the Atlas crane have both proved invaluable at major incidents, and the remains of the Scania artic are visual proof that the truck, although now showing its age, is still hard at work for its new owner.

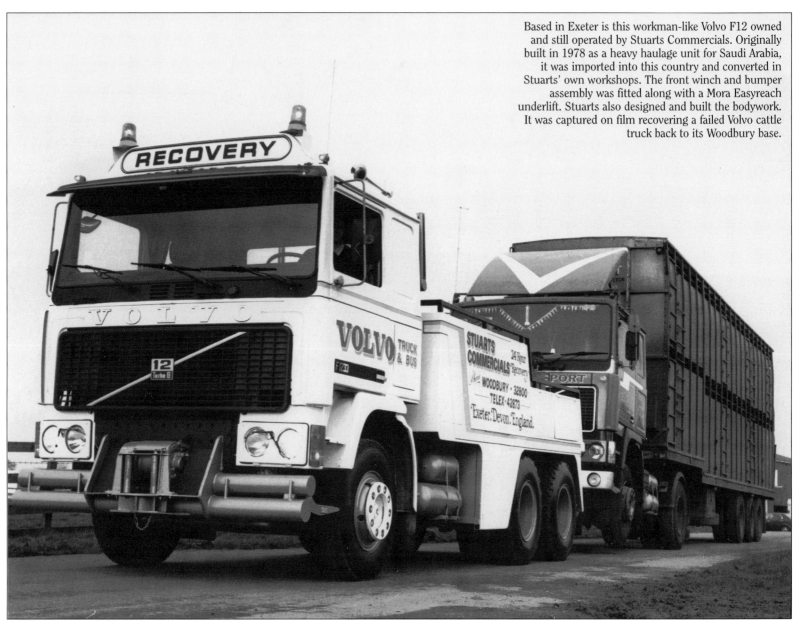

Based in Exeter is this workman-like Volvo F12 owned and still operated by Stuarts Commercials. Originally built in 1978 as a heavy haulage unit for Saudi Arabia, it was imported into this country and converted in Stuarts' own workshops. The front winch and bumper assembly was fitted along with a Mora Easyreach underlift. Stuarts also designed and built the bodywork. It was captured on film recovering a failed Volvo cattle truck back to its Woodbury base.

Right: The Cowan Motor Group were UK concessionaires for the entire range of Bro recovery equipment. To demonstrate the 200A model, they had this F12 kitted out with a full curvilinear body and operated it in their own fleet. The 200A is lifted by two hydraulic rams which sit underneath the main boom, one behind the other, unlike other twin ram installations which follow the more common side by side pattern.

Below right: Grangeside's Volvo FL233 is fitted with a Willinghams crane and body, and is one of several Willinghams equipped vehicles run by the Runcorn-based company.

Below: Starting life as a 4x2 tractor unit, Bridge Garage's Volvo was sent to Autylifts of Dewsbury, where the chassis was extended and the second lift axle added, before work began on constructing the 10 ton underlift. Two Darlington winches were added and then the stylish bodywork built. Worthy of note is the flyer which supports the beacons and the work lights. On this truck, it is angled towards the rear of the vehicle instead of the front, as is the norm. The reason for this is to enable the lights to illuminate the work area when coupling up in the dark.

Left: Every August, the annual Trans-Pennine vintage commercial vehicle rally culminates in a large gathering on the Stray at Harrogate. After a downpour in 1993, many low loaders, used to ferry participants to the event, became bogged down and unable to move. Highway Recovery have for years provided emergency back up for the event and were soon busy winching the unfortunate vehicles onto firm ground using their Concept-equipped F12.

Below left: This FH16 Globetrotter is by today's standards quite rare in that it has only two axles. Most of today's recovery vehicles are built on three or four axle chassis but these can prove expensive to operate on lightweight jobs such as 7.5 tonne vehicles or solo tractor units, so some operators still find there is work for the light two axle recovery truck. This was photographed outside the Boniface factory in Norfolk shortly after being completed.

Below: A standard cabbed FH12 6x4 belonging to Kenfield Recovery. Fitted with super single front tyres, extra roof mounted lights and a very shiny paint finish, this again has been equipped by Boniface with an Interstater and twin winches. The double drive rear bogie is air suspended.

Our final look at the FH Volvo is of S & H's Volvo FH12 photographed in April 1997 at the B.P. Truckstop, Alconbury, near Cambridge. Seen attending an ailing FH Volvo from the Brian Yeardley fleet, L676 GBW is rather unique. It is of 8x2 configuration and it is possible to raise the second and third axles clear of the ground. The chassis was modified by S & H before being dispatched to Boniface for the Recoverer crane and bodywork to be fitted.

Above: First operated by the U.S. Army, when it was fitted with bridge laying equipment, this White 6x6 now carries recovery equipment built by Burrows of Borrowash. The extending jib is raised by two rams that were removed from a quarry dump truck. With a maximum speed of 30 mph, special jobs only are the order of the day.

Left above: Equipment manufacturers are always pleased when one of their units enters the fleet of one of the larger motoring organisations. J & J Conversions of Andover equipped this VW LT50 with their Inter City spec lift on behalf of the RAC. The crew cab only has one access door, this being placed on the nearside. The reason for this is to prevent passengers getting out of the cab in front of moving traffic.

Left: Robert Wynn & Sons took advantage of the availability of surplus Allied military vehicles after World War Two as proven by their almost legendary Pacific and Diamond T heavy haulage units. Also added to the fleet in 1947 were a number of Ward Le France and Federal wreckers, as well as being employed on recovery work they provided support and assistance to other aspects of the company's activities as illustrated here in 1950 when a 40 ton Butane vessel was being moved on-site at the Llandarcy Oil Refinery.

RECOVERY TECHNIQUES - SLIDE BACK VEHICLES

One of the most complex types of light recovery vehicles is the slide-back or semi demountable type. First developed to cater for the transportation of items of construction plant, its adaptability for vehicle recovery was soon realised.

The slide-back is a hydraulically operated system which tilts and slides the vehicle body until it touches the floor and forms a ramp. The casualty can then be driven or winched aboard and made safe whilst the body is slid back up its subframe, lowered back onto the trucks chassis and locked down. The final stage is to secure the vehicle being transported , in readiness for the journey.

The greatest advantage of this system is that no matter how badly damaged a vehicle maybe, and they can sometimes be beyond recognition, one man can recover the vehicle with ease.

Left: The recovery vehicle is positioned in front of the casualty.

Below left: The deck is tilted hydraulically and slid backwards to form a ramp, up which the casualty is then winched.

Below: The deck slides back up its subframe and is lowered to the chassis. The casualty is then secured and transported away.

RECOVERY TECHNIQUES - THE UNDERLIFT

Today's changes in commercial vehicle engineering and design have paved the way for the mass acceptance of the underlift or damage free recovery crane.

Right: The recovery vehicle is reversed up to the casualty, leaving enough room for the bottom arm to be lowered to the floor.

Right middle: The arm is lowered and suitable attachments, (forks) are placed in the crosshead brackets.

Right lower: The arm is extended underneath the casualty until a safe place to carry out the lift is found, in this case the road springs. When the forks are positioned so as to avoid damage, the weight is taken, and the vehicle lifted until the front wheels are clear of the floor.

Below: With the extending arm retracted and locked in place, the lift is now complete and all that remains is to secure the casualty to the crosshead, fit a safety chain, disconnect the drive line, fit an auxiliary light board on the rear, release the brakes and tow it away.

INCIDENTS

Snow and ice present many problems for drivers and invariably accidents happen. It is then up to the recovery crew to rectify the situation in a professional and skilled manner.

This Foden tipper was hauling coal from a private drift mine, up the approach road to the storage yard when it succumbed to a track that was a sheet of ice. The result was a ditched truck blocking the only road into and out of the moorland pit.

The recovery truck was reversed nearly a mile to the site as there was no room to get past or turn round. A winch equipped tractor was placed in the field in order to give a sideways pull and a tunnel was dug on the nearside of the tipper to allow a strop to be anchored around a road spring. The combine pull of the tractor and the Mercedes, plus the icy track resulted in the tipper being extracted.

Although it sounds easy, the extreme cold and the driving wind made conditions for the crew less than favourable, nevertheless, the job was completed to the relief of all concerned.

Left above and left: The Foden loaded with 15 tons of coal in the ditch and the nearside view, prior to the access tunnel being dug for the strop.

Below: With the tractor in the field and the Mercedes both providing a sideways pull, the Foden emerges from the ditch.

Left lower: The light is now fading and the temperature dropping to well below zero as the Foden is winched to the top of the road and away from danger.

INCIDENTS

The Lancashire town of Baxenden is home to one of the north's most famous meat pie manufacturers, Walter Holland and Sons.

The factory freezer units are cooled by water fed into the plant from a lodge which at one time was unfenced. This lodge was surrounded by a sloping vehicle park and, on two separate occasions, vehicles have found their way into the lodge. Both were recovered using the same method, and both involved the author getting his feet wet.

Right and below: Eighteen months apart, a Ford Cargo and a Bedford TK go for a swim.

Below middle: The author wades out and attaches lifting chains to the front towing eyes so the vehicle can be lifted clear by means of a crane.

Below right: With the vehicle lifted clear of the bottom, chains are secured round the front axle and the truck is winched from its watery grave.

Opposite: The truck is winched up the banking and back onto the vehicle park.

INCIDENTS

Curtain sided vehicles and tilt trailers are notoriously unstable in windy conditions, their sides acting like giant sails, often with disastrous consequences. Such was the case here, where a gust of wind blew this M.A.N artic off-course, causing it to demolish a dry stone wall and career through a farm gate. When the vehicle finally came to rest, the trailer wheels were left balancing precariously over a drop into the field.

Right: The artic comes to rest , the damage caused can be clearly seen.

Below: The area is made safe and the twin boom manoeuvred alongside the stricken trailer to provide a sideways pull later on.

Right lower: The crew set about securing a strop around the trailer which will be used to pull it back onto the road. The underlift is positioned so as to lift the wheels clear of the wall. Fortunately the trailer was empty and had a substantial under run bumper.

Right bottom: With the trailer now back on the road, the whole outfit can now be winched clear of the gate and made ready for the recovery home.

INCIDENTS

Accidents that can be attributed to your own carelessness are bad enough, but when it is caused by someone else's sheer stupidity, it can be downright annoying. This unlucky driver was forced to take severe evasive action when an oncoming motorist decided to overtake another vehicle when there simply was not room to do so. The result was his Leyland, on its side in a ditch, minus its load of steel coils and the perpetrator speeding off into the distance.

Left: The forlorn vehicle lying in the ditch.

Right below: A side pull from the Holmes 750 stands the vehicle back on its wheels, then the recovery vehicle is moved to a side road at the end of the ditch; considerably safer than on the main carriageway. Cables are fed out to the casualty whilst the local constabulary give the crew as much safety cover as possible.

Below and bottom right: The casualty is winched along the ditch. As the Leyland leaves the ditch, it is coupled up for the journey home.

INCIDENTS

Right: Recovery crews not only have to deal with a stricken vehicle but are sometimes entrusted with the task of removing the load as well. This load of waste paper was on its way to a pulping mill when the accident occurred. A telephone call to the works manager soon had specialist equipment dispatched in line with their own emergency procedure; the waste was cleared away in under an hour.

Right lower: A lapse of concentration, a brush with the kerb, and a few seconds later it is all over. That's what happened with this Bedford tipper. The resulting accident ripped the front axle completely off the truck, caused severe damage to the cab and demolished a large section of dry stone wall. The three man crew all escaped unscathed.

Below: Treacherous road conditions and falling sleet, all contributed to this accident. The Ford Cargo has left the road, demolished a section of armco barrier and is teetering at the top of a 60 foot drop into a stream. Both the cab and chassis have sustained severe impact damage. The vehicle was recovered by building steps out of wooden blocks sited behind the front wheels. As the truck was winched backwards, it climbed the steps clearing the flattened barrier before coming slowly back onto the road.

INCIDENTS

Left: Burnley Council's refuse vehicle moved over to allow another vehicle to pass and ended up in this ditch. It was recovered by passing a strop over the body and securing a chain to the rear axle. Whilst one winch from the twin boom pulled on the strop and rolled the truck out of the ditch, the other winch pulled it back onto the road. This type of recovery is when the twin boom comes into its own, with its ability to work both booms and winches independently.

Below left: Some of the most challenging recoveries are of pieces of plant machinery which tend to work off the beaten track. This JCB was dredging a fishing club lodge when the workings flooded, causing the machine to sink and list profusely. Vehicular access was impossible so another machine was brought in to dig away underneath the stricken JCB until it was able to stand upright. With water still entering the workings, the machine came to rest with just the cab showing, so a complex arrangement of cables and snatch blocks was rigged up and the machine was extracted using a tractor equipped with a 10 ton Boughton winch. It was the complexity of the rigging that made this possible.

Below: This Ford Cargo was tipping its load of soil, at the top of a 200 feet drop into a river, when the edge of the roadway collapsed sending the little tipper plummeting down the hill side. Fortunately for the driver, who was sitting in the cab at the time, the vehicle was fitted with a Hiab crane. This had been raised into the air to allow the body to be tipped and stopped the truck from rolling right over.

INCIDENTS

Right: A phone call requesting the recovery of a car weighing 6 tons was greeted with slight suspicion but upon arrival at the scene all was made clear. It was an armoured car which had been bought by a private individual for use in the sport of paint balling. Whilst negotiating a quarry approach road, the owner had lost control and finished up at the bottom of a fifty foot ravine. The Bedford based vehicle had been in service with the Swedish Civil Defence Authority and was designed for riot control duties, it was duly winched out of the ravine and towed to it's destination.

Below right: A misjudged approach to a building site saw this Ford D Series disappear into a stream, leaving the front wheels some four feet in the air. The load of cement was unloaded before the truck was winched back onto the track without further damage.

Below: Failing to negotiate a bend at the bottom of a steep hill resulted in this refuse vehicle rolling over and demolishing the kitchen of a terraced house. Miraculously, the crew escaped with only minor injuries. Recovery is about to commence and as can be seen, the prop shaft has been removed prior to righting the vehicle. This is done to prevent damage to the automatic gearbox when towing the wreck away, and is easier to do when the truck is lying on its side.

RECOVERY VEHICLES in Colour

This Mammoth Major Mk III belonged to Cedars Autos of West London. Unusual in being an 8x2 configuration with the drive going to the rear axle, it has the Reynolds Boughton twin boom crane which never gained the same popularity as the Holmes model that it mirrors. Photographed in 1973, the vehicle carries a registered index number and does not appear to be operating under trade plates which was the normal practice at that time. The presence of axles under the booms suggests the vehicle may be returning from a breaker's yard to prepare for fitment of the parts to a customer's vehicle.

Above: Newtyle purchased this ex M.o.D. AEC Mammoth Major which had served as a fuel bowser with the RAF. Owner Al0n Sime simply removed the tank and metering equipment, installed a Holmes 750 and put the vehicle to work and the result is an extremely well turned out vehicle.

146

Above: Ivan Chant's 8x4 Autocar came to the UK in the early Eighties having previously served in the fleet of Howard Kauff of Florida. The Holmes 850 equipped truck soon became a regular sight on roads and country lanes around its Frome, Somerset base where its owner ran Berkley Commercial Vehicle Repairs. Weighing in at over 20 tons and over 30' long, the Cummins-powered monster is fitted with the largest of the Holmes twin boom cranes and has dual controls fitted to either side of the bodywork. Ivan has since retired and the truck has been sold on.

148

Left: This Bedford TM 3800 of Cannon Commercials, Newton Abbot, equipped with a Holmes 650 crane was recovering this Bovey Tracey-based Iveco-Ford van of T Quality Ltd when photographed on a decidedly wet day, on the A38 overpass near its base in 1987. It was previously with Skippers of Gloucester and has since been sold on.

Above: This DAF 2800 of South West Motors of Taunton, Somerset, is rated for 55 tonnes gtw and equipped with an early example of the Interstater underlift. The recovery unit - originally an artic tractor - worked in the London area before being brought west in 1989 by Mike and Merv Wadham. After refurbishment by their staff, it began a new life in their vehicle recovery and repair business.

Left: Saunders of Hemel Hempstead operated this Diamond T for many years. It is seen here in October 1967 and is fitted with a Gar-Wood twin boom which fitted perfectly inside the original ballast box.

Above: Steadplans other vehicle is this LV cabbed example. Believed to have come from the fleet of David Crouch, the Cummins engined variant is an ex heavy haulage tractor unit and is fitted with the Dominator 30 recovery crane.

151

Beresford of Stoke-on-Trent were long time ERF customers and ran several MV steel cabbed tractor units in their fleet. Like many own account recovery vehicles, a covered workshop area was included in the design which enabled roadside repairs to be carried out, with recovery being a last resort.

Originally built as an 8x4 tipper, this ERF was purchased by J & K Recovery after a lost contract forced its original owners to sell the truck. The conversion from tipper to recovery unit was carried out by Worldwide Recovery Systems who fitted a 50/30 T3DWX Century underlift with a 15 ton extending top boom and two 15 ton winches. Powered by a 350 Cummins celect engine, the EC10, whose regular driver is Anthony McFadden, is based in Leighton Buzzard, Bedfordshire. J & K run a 40 plus fleet of recovery units, these operating out of three depots covering all parts of the UK and the Continent.

Above: Heavy Transport's Foden S20 began life in 1960 as a heavy haulage unit for Western Excavating (ECC). Its main purpose was the movement of plant on site or to and from Midlands-based manufacturers. In the late Sixties it was withdrawn from service to be converted, in-house, into a recovery vehicle before being liveried in Heavy Transport colours. The fabricated jib rests on a steel bar slotted through a series of holes in the upright mast and lifting is carried out by the cable drum from the Darlington winch behind the cab being fed over a pulley at the end of the jib. Note the provision on the front bumper for extra ballast to keep the front wheels on the ground during heavy lifting. The Foden still exists and is being restored by a Gloucester enthusiast.

154

Above: Les Wallings' eight wheeled Foden recovery unit, again prior to the design changes with the abandonment of the demountable subframe concept and a full curvilinear body fitted. An impressive vehicle enhanced by the Preston-based company's stylish, yet tasteful livery.

Left: The west Dorset coastline provides a suitable backdrop for this former development vehicle from the British Army's Medium Mobility recovery unit programme. The Foden operates out of Jim Frodsham's Morecombelake garage on specialist recovery work through out the South West.

Above: Seen demonstrating its capabilities with this Leyland Medium Mobility support vehicle is the Foden Ekalift 2500 Recovery unit. It has been designed for recovery of the heaviest of the Army's wheeled transport including the Improved Medium Mobility Load Carrier (IMMLC) based on the same 8x6 Foden chassis.

Left: This Ford Cargo 1313 recovery unit was previously owned by Securicor and operated by the company out of its Plymouth facility. Now in the colours of Ricky Gaunt's Field Services, also Plymouth based, the unit is pictured in January 1998 having recovered this Iveco Ford box van that was involved in an accident on the A379 near Kingsbridge, South Devon.

Above: Another adaption of an Iveco twin steer unit is this example of Bookham Commercials who specialised in international truck salvage, the lhd Iveco 220-30 tractor unit is fitted with a Mk 1 Interstater underlift and a 10 ton Dp winch. Although an unusual axle configuration for a recovery vehicle, it was deemed adequate for its owner's needs. Bookham's now trade under a different name.

Left: Over 25 years old and looking resplendent is Plymouth City Bus's Leyland Hippo. Fitted with the traditional covered work area bodywork and a Harvey Frost crane, this truck looks every inch a working vehicle. The body appears to be fitted with a detachable panel which suggest that the crane can slew round to the side, a function available on this type of crane. Note that the sides of the jib have been panelled giving a smoother, cleaner appearance.

Above: Seen climbing the alpine course at the Fighting Vehicle Research & Development Establishment (FVRDE), Bagshot, Surrey in June 1969, is the then resident heavy recovery vehicle, A civilian registered Leyland 6x6. Popularly known as the 'Martian, some 280 were built for the British Army, being equipped with recovery equipment built by the Royal Ordnance Factories in conjunction with Leyland Motors.

Above: D & C Fry's Mack Interstater came from the fleet of West Scotland Excavations Ltd where it was engaged in haulage of plant from the company's Coatbridge base. Roger Dyson fitted the Enforcer recovery gear and this vehicle became yet another example of an Aerodyne-cabbed FM Mack moving from the world of heavy haulage to that of heavy recovery.

Right: The multitude of brackets and fitments supplied with BRO and EKA cranes is to allow the recovery of virtually all wheeled vehicles that exist. Seen here on Wards Renault is a crane pulley attachment that fits into the end of the extending arm in place of the cross-head. This type of crane is sometimes referred to as the 'wishbone' type due to the shape of the main jib.

Above: Scratchwood Services in the Autumn of 1974 is the setting for this impressive Scammell Constructor belonging to the London Brick Company of Stewartby, Beds. The unit, equipped with a TFL T20 crane, has just carried out a front lift on one of the company's Mk V AECs.

Right: This Scammell S26 began its working life as a heavy haulage unit with Tony Morgan of Brigend. Acquired in 1992 by Taunton Trucks, it was modified and extended in their workshops. The Holmes 750 equipment being transferred from the company's previous recovery vehicle, an AEC.

LEYLAND DAF

Taunton Trucks Ltd. 0823 - 331275

Leyland DAFaid
FREEPHONE
0800 919395

Leyland DAF
BACK-UP

SCAMMELL

Taunton Trucks

350 CHARGECOOLED
400 BHP

C667 JKG

165

Above: This unit, featured at an M1 service area, is one of a large fleet operated by Kenfield Motors Recovery of Pump Lane, Hayes, Middlesex. The Scania is fitted with a Boniface underlift and Active Air Suspension which allows the third axle to lift as illustrated here. A workmanlike vehicle with a livery to match.

Above: Photographed in May 1996 is Kings Ferry of Gillingham's Volvo F88 recovery unit. The coach, one of a fifty strong fleet, had broke down in Scotland and was in the process of being towed south to the company's Kent base by the Harvey Frost equipped unit. The F88 began life as an artic unit in the early 70s.

Above: This unusual wrecker operated by Commercial Motors in 1969 was a Thornycroft PKQR6 with an AEC Mk V grille grafted on. The chassis terminated immediately beyond the driving axles and a hydraulically elevated single-piece girder boom was mounted. Chains secured the vehicle being recovered.

168